GOUZAO GONGJI

MASTER HEI LONG

GOUZAO GONGJI

SEVEN NEUROLOGICAL ATTACKS FOR INFLICTING SERIOUS DAMAGE

PALADIN PRESS
BOULDER, COLORADO

Also by Master Hei Long:

Advanced Dragon's Touch
Da Zhimingde: Striking Deadly Blows to Vital Organs
Dragons Touch: Weaknesses of the Human Anatomy
Gouzao Gongji: Seven Neurological Attacks for Inflicting Serious Damage
Guge Gongji: Seven Primary Targets to Take Anyone Out of a Fight
Iron Hand of the Dragon's Touch: Secrets of Breaking Power
Master's Guide to Basic Self-Defense: Progressive Retraining of the Reflexive Response

Gouzao Gongji: Seven Neurological Attacks for Inflicting Serious Damage
by Master Hei Long

Copyright © 1992 by Master Hei Long

ISBN 0-87364-692-4
Printed in the United States of America

Published by Paladin Press, a division of
Paladin Enterprises, Inc.
Gunbarrel Tech Center
7077 Winchester Circle
Boulder, Colorado 80301 USA
+1.303.443.7250

Direct inquiries and/or orders to the above address.

PALADIN, PALADIN PRESS, and the "horse head" design are trademarks belonging to Paladin Enterprises and registered in United States Patent and Trademark Office.

All rights reserved. Except for use in a review, no portion of this book may be reproduced in any form without the express written permission of the publisher.

Neither the author nor the publisher assumes any responsibility for the use or misuse of information contained in this book.

Visit our Web site at www.paladin-press.com

Contents

Chapter One
1 THE SEVEN PRIMARY TARGETS 1

Chapter Two
15 DIRECTIONS OF FORCE 15

Chapter Three
27 SINGLE-KICK RETURNS 27

Chapter Four
61 SINGLE-PUNCH RETURNS 61

Chapter Five
97 COMBINATION KICKS 97

Chapter Six
137 HAND COMBINATIONS 137

CHAPTER ONE

THE SEVEN PRIMARY TARGETS

The seven primary targets upon which this study will focus are named and exhibited in their anatomical locations in Figures 1 and 2. A brief word about the physiological nature of this set of targets is in order at this point.

Primarily, attacks on these targets are attacks on the central nervous system. The base of the cranium and tip of the mandible directly affect the brain. The ears focus on a higher cerebellar function, and the brachial plexus, median, and radial nerves directly affect the nervous system itself, central and peripheral respectively. An attack on the solar plexus is the exception. Though it is a neurological attack, the effect is upon a visceral organ: the diaphragm.

There is a marked contrast between these targets and those that were studied in *Guge Gongji* (available from Paladin Press) and those that will be studied in *Da Zhimingde* when it is published. An effective attack on the targets upon which *Guge Gongji* focused will do serious structural damage to an opponent. One of the targets in that study is potentially lethal. In *Da Zhimingde*, two targets are critical and five are lethal. The targets studied in

Gouzao Gongji lie comfortably between the two: serious enough to stop an opponent of comparable size, strength, and weight.

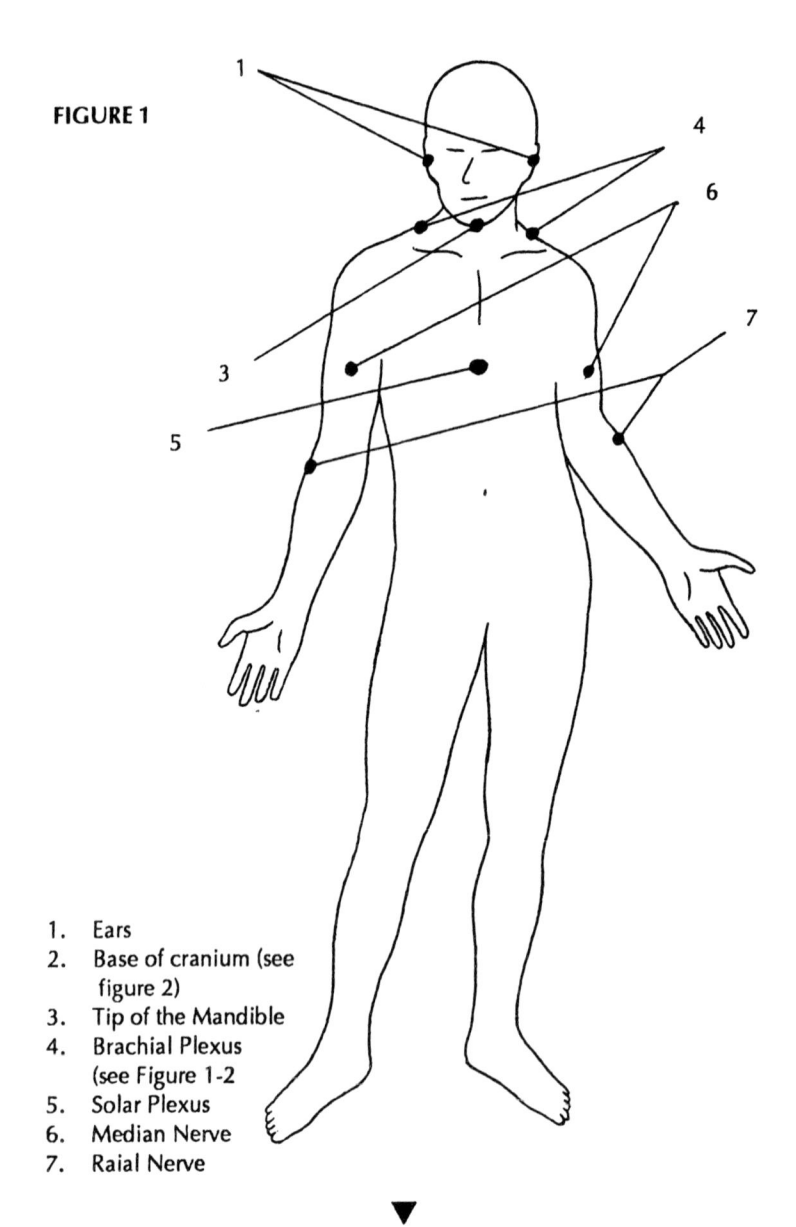

FIGURE 1

1. Ears
2. Base of cranium (see figure 2)
3. Tip of the Mandible
4. Brachial Plexus (see Figure 1-2)
5. Solar Plexus
6. Median Nerve
7. Raial Nerve

Together, these three texts will provide a comfortable range of targets from which to choose, according to the dangers involved with particular opponents.

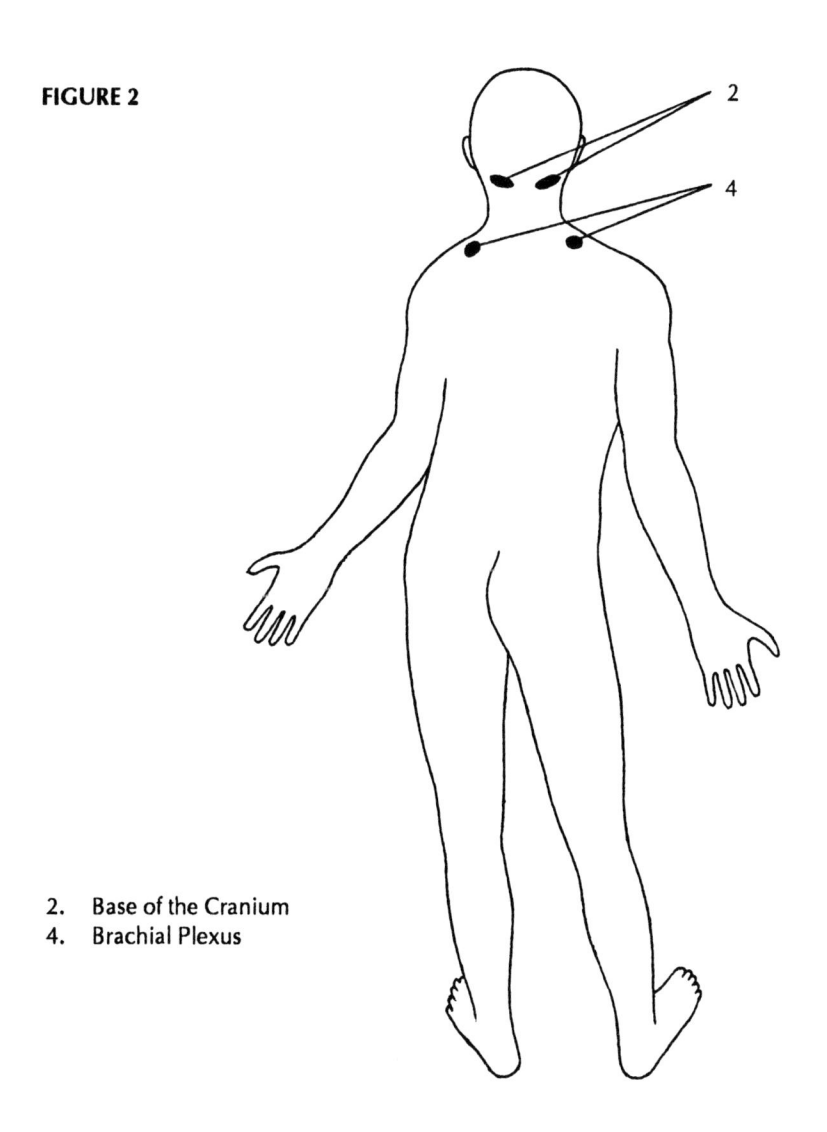

FIGURE 2

2. Base of the Cranium
4. Brachial Plexus

▼

Target Number 1: Ears

Think for a moment about your ears. What thoughts come to mind? They are protrusions on each side of the head. If there is the least bit of vanity in your personality, they may be either too large or too small. Finally, you might consider one of their sensory functions—hearing.

One of the physiological functions of the ear includes the sensory reception of sound. Sound waves travel down the external acoustic meatus and cause vibrations which affect the tympanic membrane, more commonly referred to as the eardrum (see fig. 3). These vibrations are transmitted by neural pathways to the brain, where they are deciphered and matched with the memory for identification. This function is, of course, a crucial one, but it is insignificant when compared to the function of the inner ear.

Deep within the ear lies the "inner ear." Anatomically, the innermost part of the inner ear is composed of four primary parts: the posterior ampulla, the superior ampulla, the saccule, and the utricle. The inner ear is the sensory receptor for equilibrium. It is constantly receiving and

FIGURE 3

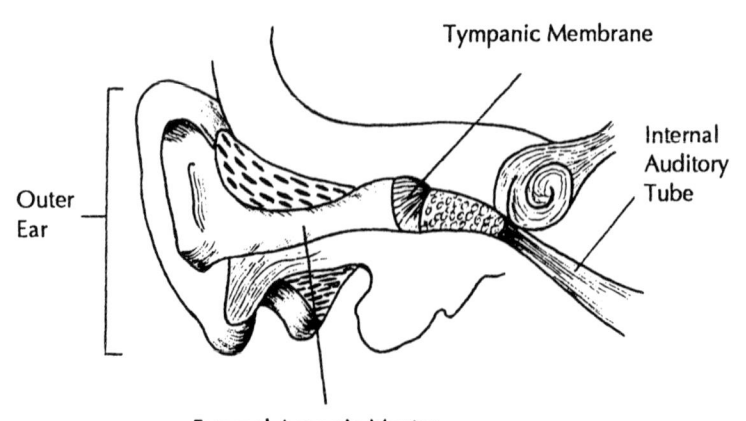

Tympanic Membrane

Internal Auditory Tube

Outer Ear

External Acoustic Meatus

▼

transmitting data on posture and the position of the head. This data is transmitted to the cerebellum, where motor centers maintain posture and equilibrium.

Consider balance for walking, ascending or descending a staircase, or reaching for an object. Do you constantly think about balancing yourself? If you step improperly or one of your feet slips, do you always fall, or does your body react and correct the imbalance with another step or a shift in your body position? These corrections are made by the cerebral motor centers of the brain, based on the information received from the inner ear.

The ear, then, is a critical target. If striking the ear can disrupt balance, then the nucleus of physical combat is broken, for without balance, the body is virtually useless as a fighting machine. Properly striking the ear, which will be discussed in the following chapter, will render a high level of pain and disrupt vital physiological functions.

Target Number 2: Base of the Cranium

As a target, the base of the cranium offers choices as to the severity of an attack. The cervical vertebrae (discussed as Target Number 7 in *Guge Gongji*, pp. 30-36) meet the cranial base at its centermost point in the neck. We will not repeat the analysis of the cervical vertebrae here. Our areas of concentration in this study will be the two points indicated in Figure 2: the base of the cranium and the brachial plexus.

Reach back with your right hand and place your second and third fingertips on the right or left area indicated in Figure 2. With the head held straight up, you will detect a depression in the area. Release your fingertips from that area and move them to the centerline of the neck at the base of the cranium. You will feel what resembles two connecting cords, between which is another smaller depression. Go to Figure 8. The two cordlike, muscular attachments are the points where the trapezius muscles meet the

▼

FIGURE 4

Cerebral Hemispheres

Cerebellum

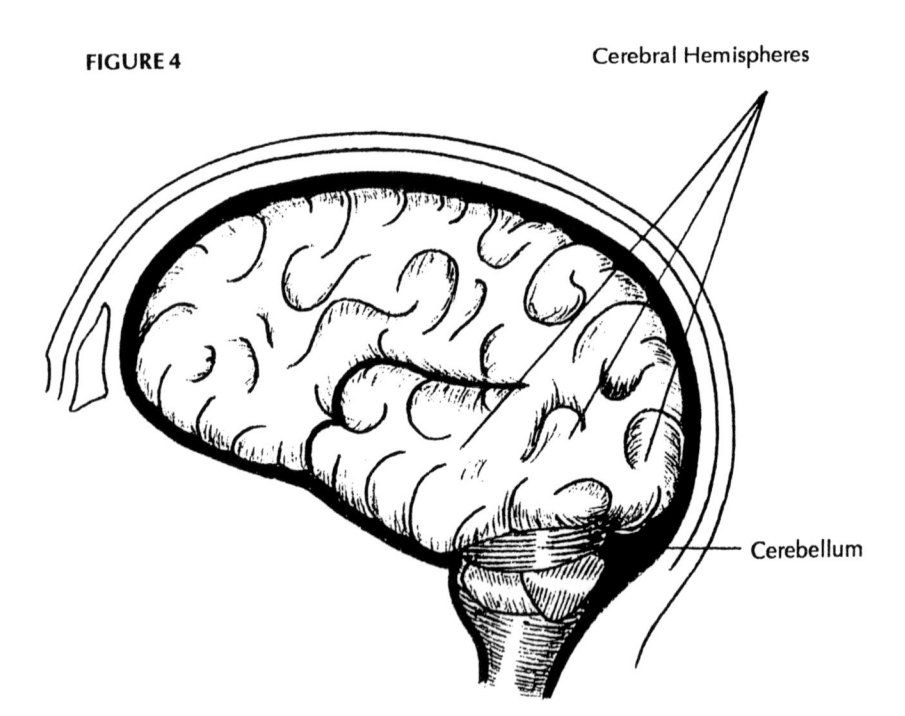

base of the cranium on each side of the centerline.

By striking into the areas indicated in Figure 2, you avoid the cushioning effect the trapezius muscle would have on the blow. There are other muscles covering the contact points, but they are relatively small and would be insignificant cushions against a high-impact blow.

Observe Figure 4. Your target consists of the cerebellum and the cerebral hemispheres. You will not be able to make direct contact with the internal targets (i.e., the cerebral hemispheres), but the shock from the blow will jar them, causing unconsciousness.

Target Number 3: Tip of the Mandible

The mandible, or jaw, is that part of the bony structure of the face which moves freely in a vertical, horizontal,

▼

FIGURE 5

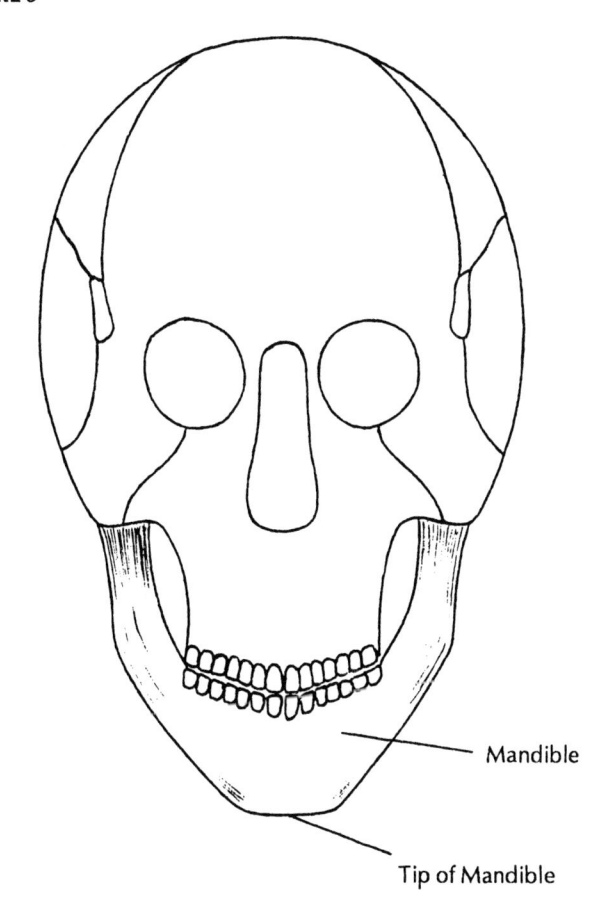

Mandible

Tip of Mandible

and circular motion. The temporomandibular joint, consisting of two condyles at the right and two at the left, holds the mandible in place while allowing the jaw freedom of movement for such simple tasks as speaking and chewing (see figs. 5 and 6).

The joints of the mandible are not weak. Their dual joint processes and their structure are firm, strong connecting points. Their structure prohibits dislocation in any direction other than forward, but if the body of the

▼

FIGURE 6

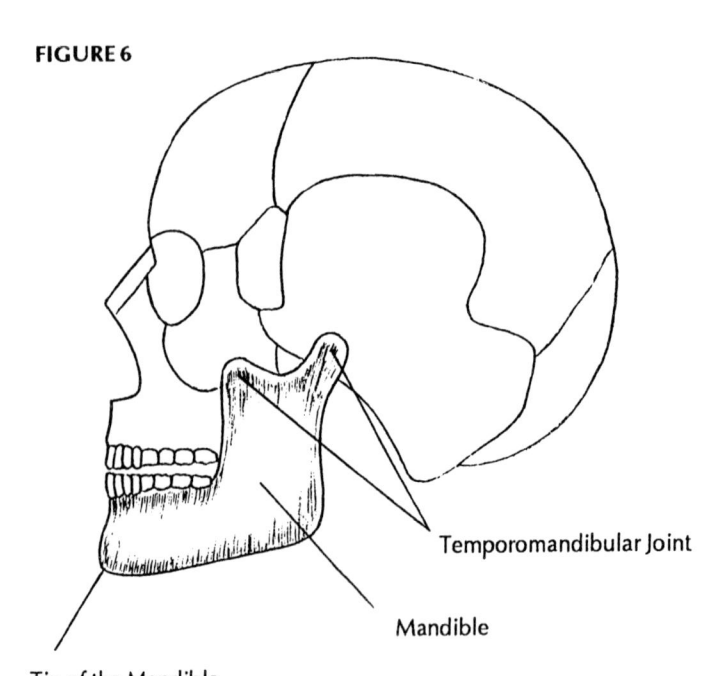

Temporomandibular Joint

Mandible

Tip of the Mandible

FIGURE 7

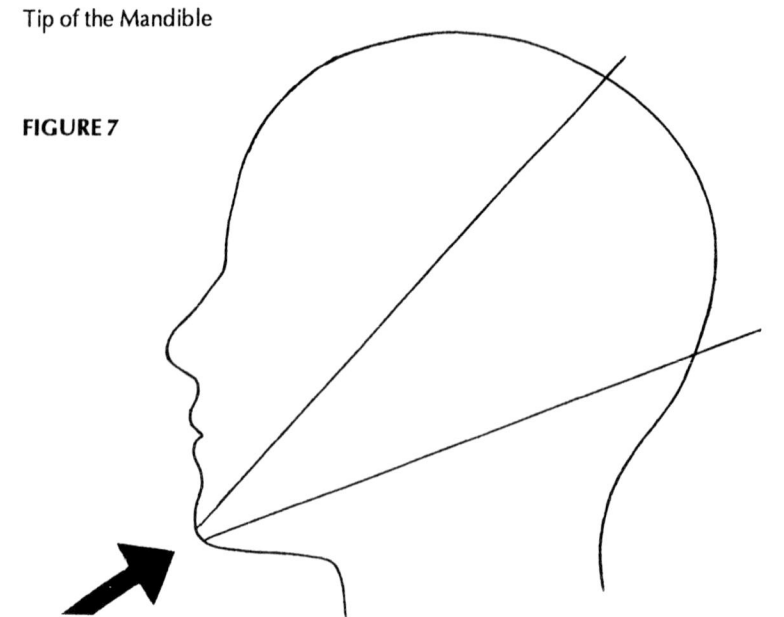

mandible or its tip is struck with an impact force sufficient to break the condyles, a high level of pain will result, along with substantial bleeding into the mouth from the rupture of the deep auricular branch of the internal maxillary artery.

Our purpose for studying the tip of the mandible as a target is for its single-stroke or "one-punch" knockout potential. Look back at Figure 4, then at Figure 7. An inclining strike, as indicated by the black arrow in Figure 7, sends a shock wave to the cerebral hemispheres. Depending on the impact force and penetration of the weapon through the target, the shock can reach as low as the medulla oblongata and as high as the frontal lobes.

The key to this target, and to the knockout potential, is the plane of the stroke. A blow that follows the plane indicated by the arrow in Figure 7 requires the least amount of force to achieve a knockout. Other angles of attack are also effective, and these will be studied in the following chapter.

Target Number 4: Brachial Plexus

The brachial plexus is a nerve complex originating from the fifth through the seventh cervical vertebrae and the first and second thoracic vertebrae. In Figure 8, the brachial plexus on the right side of the body is shown; there is an identical plexus on the left side. The nerves protruding from the foramina of these five vertebrae form the plexus and branch to a number of areas in the upper

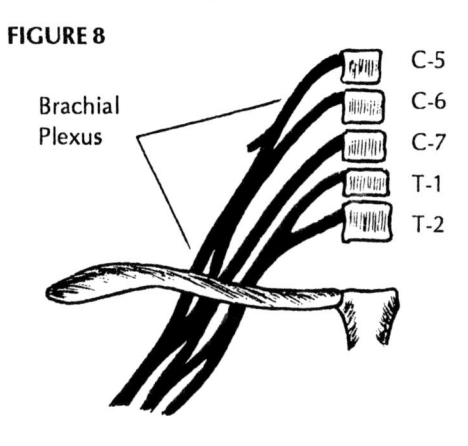

FIGURE 8

Brachial Plexus

C-5
C-6
C-7
T-1
T-2

body. (See also *Guge Gongji*, pp. 30-36). You will find another view of the brachial plexus, as its branches descend into the arm, in Figure 12.

Striking the brachial plexus with ample force will have

FIGURE 9

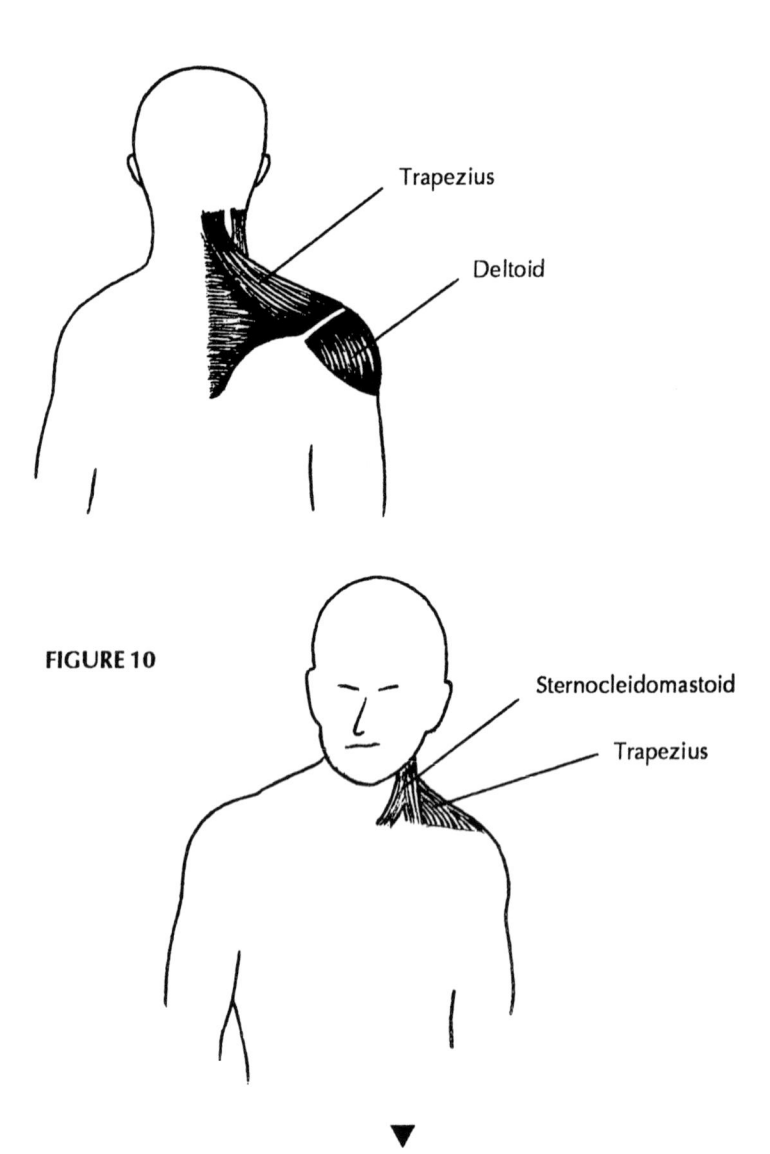

Trapezius

Deltoid

FIGURE 10

Sternocleidomastoid

Trapezius

▼

one or both of the following effects: temporary paralysis of the corresponding arm, accompanied by acute pain in the shoulder, neck, and back of the head; and unconsciousness, because of the brachial plexus' high position on the vertebral column and consequent neural connection to the cervical plexus above it.

The shoulder section of the trapezius muscle, as depicted in Figures 9 and 10, is your guide to locating the precise point of contact. Aim for the centermost point of the muscle, and with a deep, penetrating blow, you will hit your target.

Target Number 5: Solar Plexus

The solar plexus (fig. 11) is a network of nerves which supplies all the organs in the abdominal cavity. It is also known as the celiac or epigastric plexus because of its location around the celiac trunk surrounding the mesenteric artery. Nine other plexuses are tightly compacted into the immediate area. The solar plexus itself is made up of the two largest ganglia of the body: the semilunar left and the semilunar right. Its central location in front of the diaphragm and just beneath the protection of the sternum makes this target extremely vulnerable from the surface area of the body.

Like the base of the cranium, the tip of the mandible, and the brachial plexus, when struck properly, the solar plexus is a one-punch knockout target. Strikes to the base of the cranium and tip of the mandible cause unconsciousness from the application of shock to the cerebellum and the cerebral hemispheres. A strike to the brachial plexus can cause unconsciousness by stimulating the communicating cervical plexus. Impact to these targets results in unconsciousness because the brain is affected directly. With the solar plexus the effect is indirect.

When the solar plexus is struck properly with a sufficient amount of force, innervation to the abdominal viscera is interrupted. Consequently, the diaphragm ceases to

▼

FIGURE 11

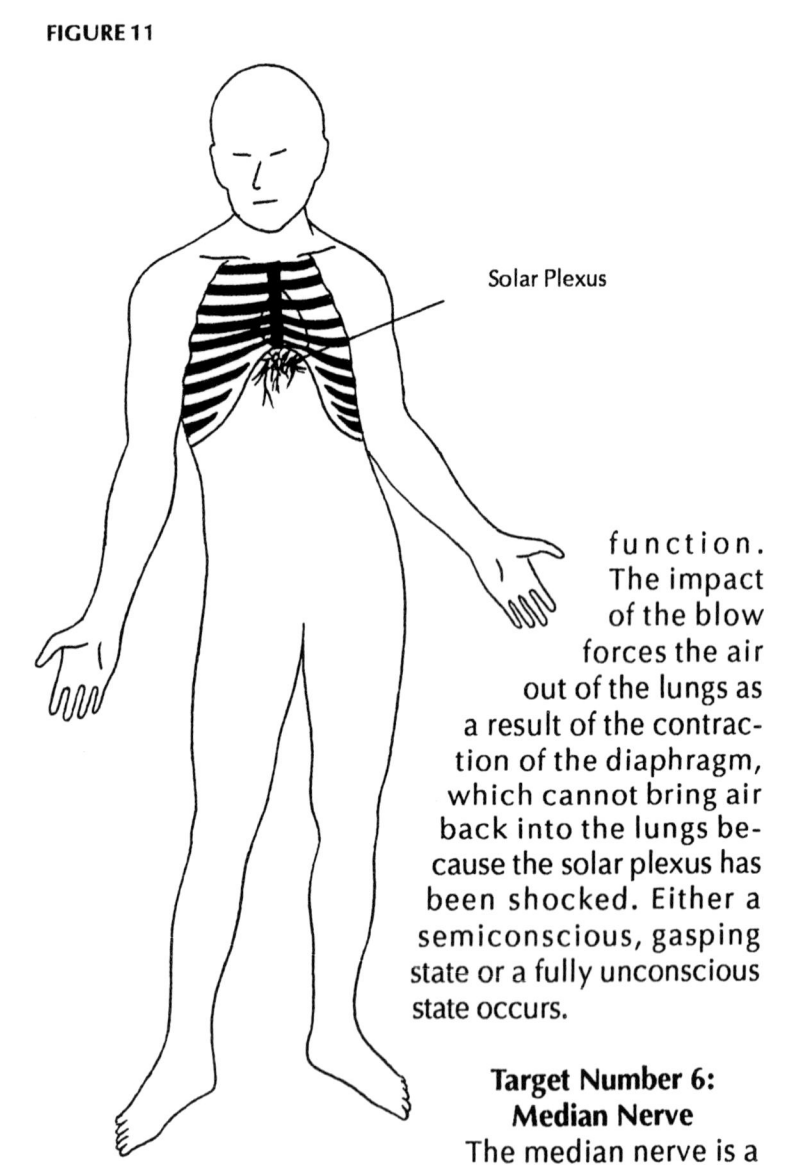

Solar Plexus

function. The impact of the blow forces the air out of the lungs as a result of the contraction of the diaphragm, which cannot bring air back into the lungs because the solar plexus has been shocked. Either a semiconscious, gasping state or a fully unconscious state occurs.

Target Number 6: Median Nerve

The median nerve is a distal branch of the brachial plexus that descends the arm beneath the biceps (fig. 12). Just as striking the brachial plexus affects the immediate area and the communicating

▼

FIGURE 12

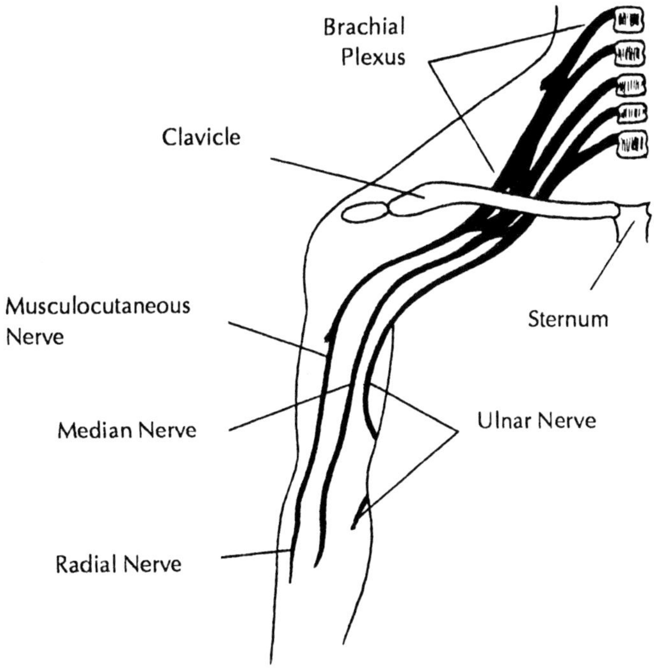
Brachial
Plexus
Clavicle
Musculocutaneous
Nerve
Sternum
Median Nerve
Ulnar Nerve
Radial Nerve

pathways below, striking the median nerve will temporarily paralyze the biceps, forearm, and hand. A high level of pain will result from a solid blow to this area as well.

Strategically, the median nerve is a preferable target when an incoming hand strike has been blocked. While an opponent's arm is extended toward you, the target area is near and very difficult to defend. A solid strike to this target will neutralize the arm, leaving the corresponding side of the body virtually defenseless.

Target Number 7: Radial Nerve

As a target, the radial nerve is primarily an acute-pain-producing pressure point. Similar to the median nerve, the

FIGURE 13

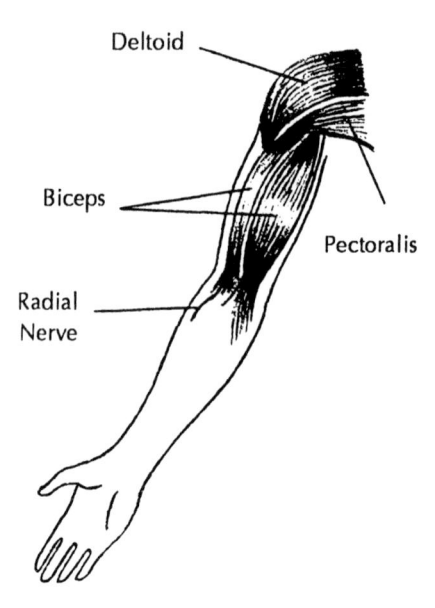

Labels: Deltoid, Biceps, Pectoralis, Radial Nerve

radial nerve is a target of convenience and availability and is often combined with an attack to the median nerve.

In Figure 13, the radial nerve is shown in its anatomical position about three inches below the fold of the arm. If you will look back at Figure 12, you will see that it is a branch of the brachial plexus descending from the musculocutaneous nerve.

▼

CHAPTER TWO

▼ ▼ ▼ ▼ ▼ ▼ ▼ ▼ ▼ ▼ ▼ ▼ ▼

DIRECTIONS OF FORCE

Iron Hand of the Dragon's Touch was a full-text study of the primary weapons of the hands and feet: how to form them, strengthen them, and develop them into hammer-hard striking apparatuses. The advantage of developing anatomical weapons is the devastating effect they have on an opponent's body—and, of course, minimization of the chance of damage to the weapons when applied to bony targets.

As you study the directions of force for these targets, you should be visualizing the anatomical weapons you would use in each instance and how to properly form and focus them. Knowing how to strike a target correctly is as necessary as knowing precisely where to strike.

Ears

Striking the ears (figs. 14 and 15) with conventional anatomical weapons has some impact on the inner ear because of the jarring effect, but your most effective weapon against the ear is either the seat of the palm or open, cupped hands. Your objective in striking this target is to trap the air in the external acoustic meatus and force it

▼

16　Gouzao Gongji　16

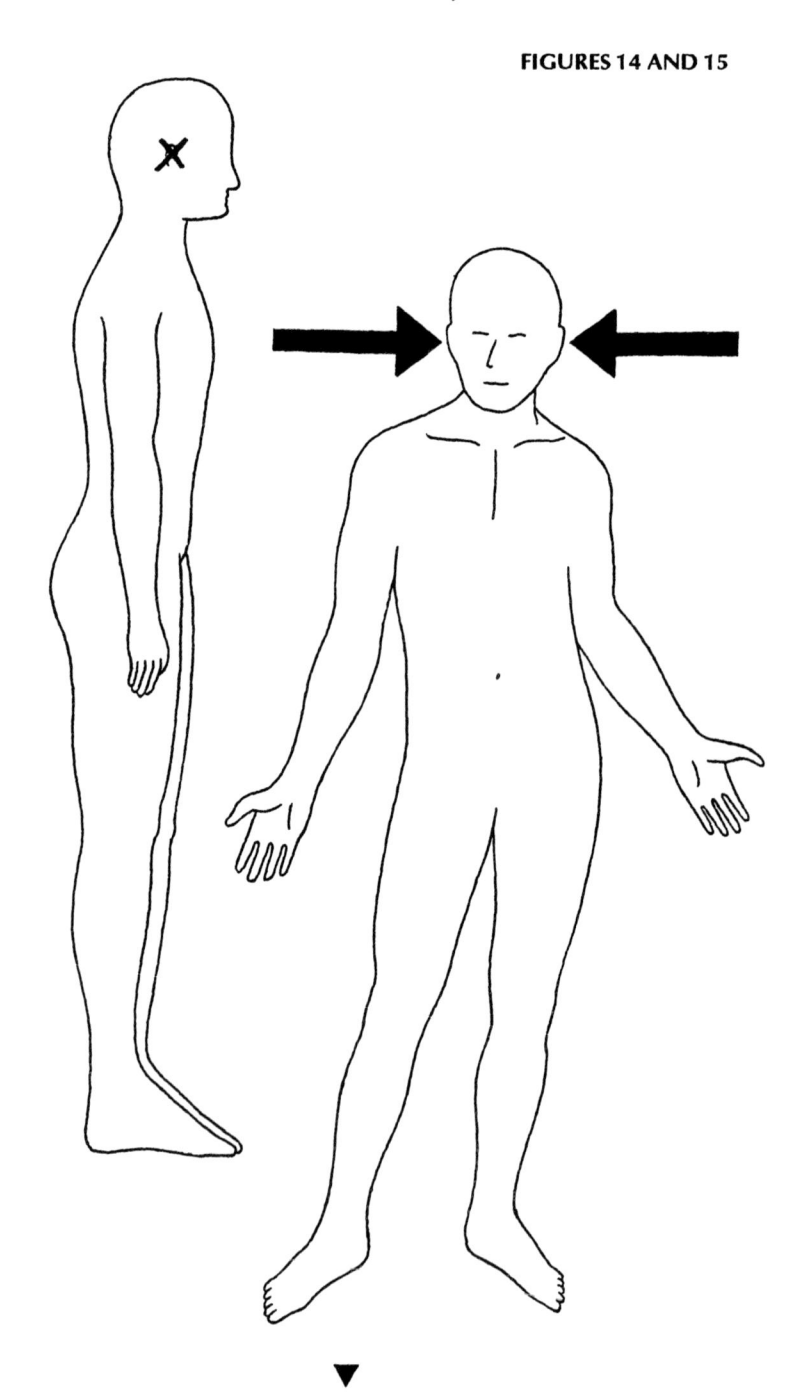

FIGURES 14 AND 15

17 DIRECTIONS OF FORCE 17

FIGURES 16 AND 17

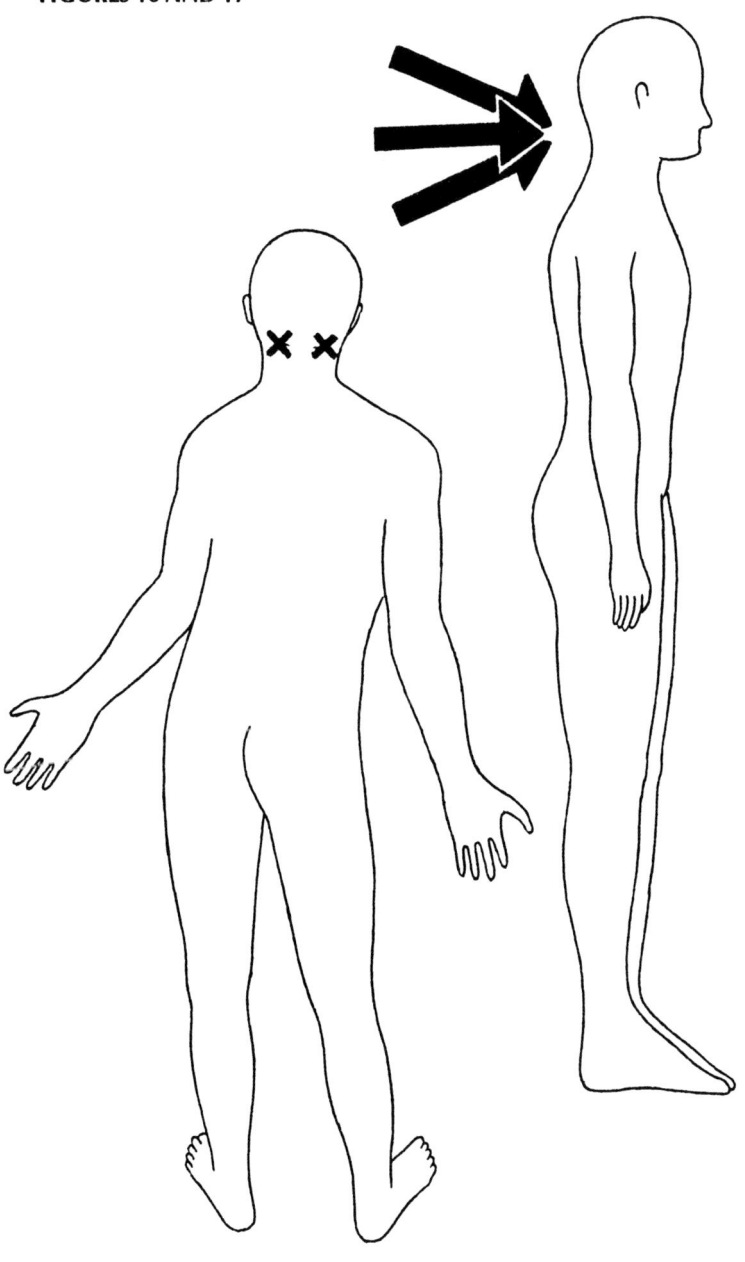

down the tube, breaking the tympanic membrane.

Your best direction of force, as indicated by the arrows in Figure 15, is horizontal, directly into the ear.

Base of the Cranium

The most potent, anatomically correct weapon with which to strike the base of the cranium (fig. 16) is the horizontal suto, in either the palm-up or palm-down position. There are three angles of attack illustrated in Figure 17. A and B will cause the cerebral shock discussed in Chapter 1. The C angle will direct the force of the blow into the first three cervical vertebrae, which could be fatal if it's a high-impact blow. The most effective angle for the knockout blow is the one depicted by arrow A.

Tip of the Mandible

Side, front, and heel-thrust kicks are excellent weapons to use against the tip of the mandible (fig. 18). Traditional straight-line and half-turn punches are also extremely effective against this target. The angle depicted by the arrow in Figure 19 is the most effective direction of force, but a deep, inclining strike would still be effective.

Brachial Plexus

Hand hammers, vertical sutos, and vertical elbows are the best weapons to apply to the brachial plexus. The inward angles depicted by the arrows in Figures 20 and 21 are preferable because they follow the natural curvature of the trapezius muscle. The arrow in Figure 22 follows the natural angle of an incoming suto or hammer.

Solar Plexus

The solar plexus, because of its lower position in the body (fig. 23), is more readily accessible to kicks than the higher targets. The front and side kicks are excellent attacks for the A and B angles (fig. 24), respectively. The

▼

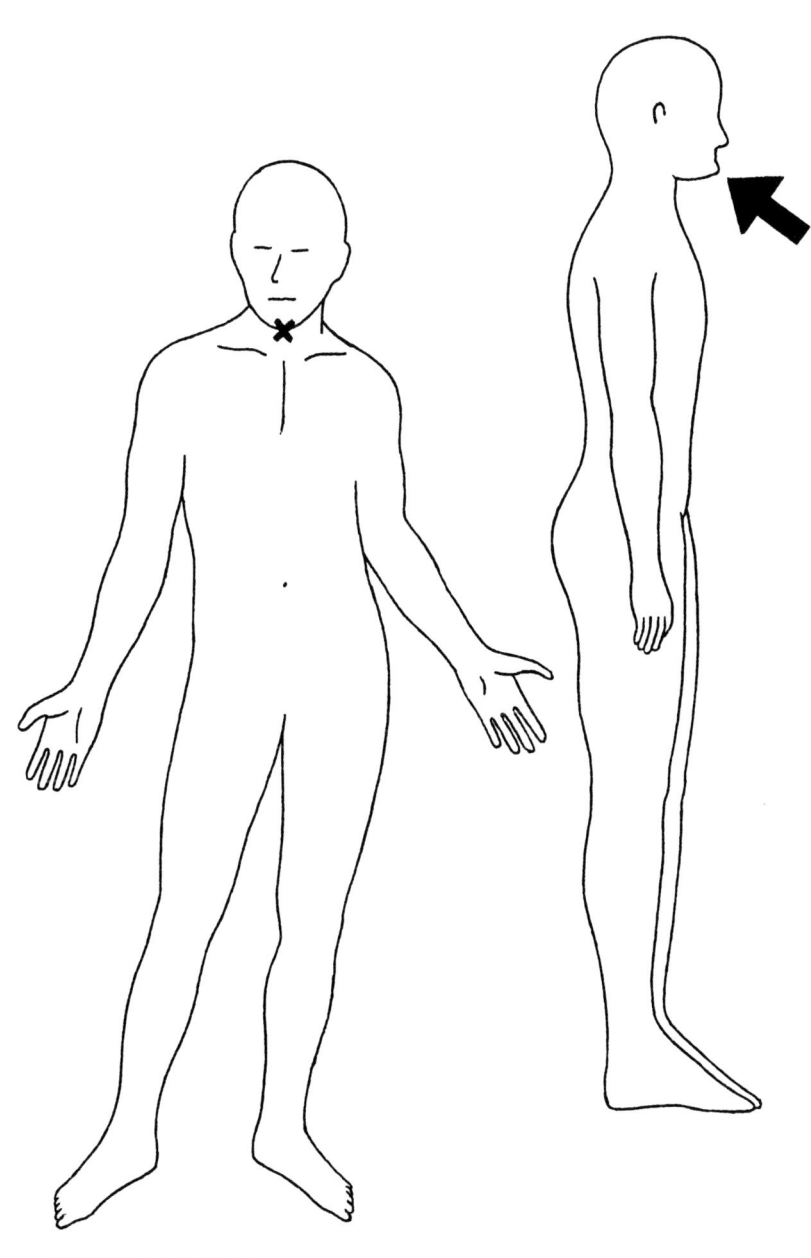

FIGURES 18 AND 19

20 GOUZAO GONGJI 20

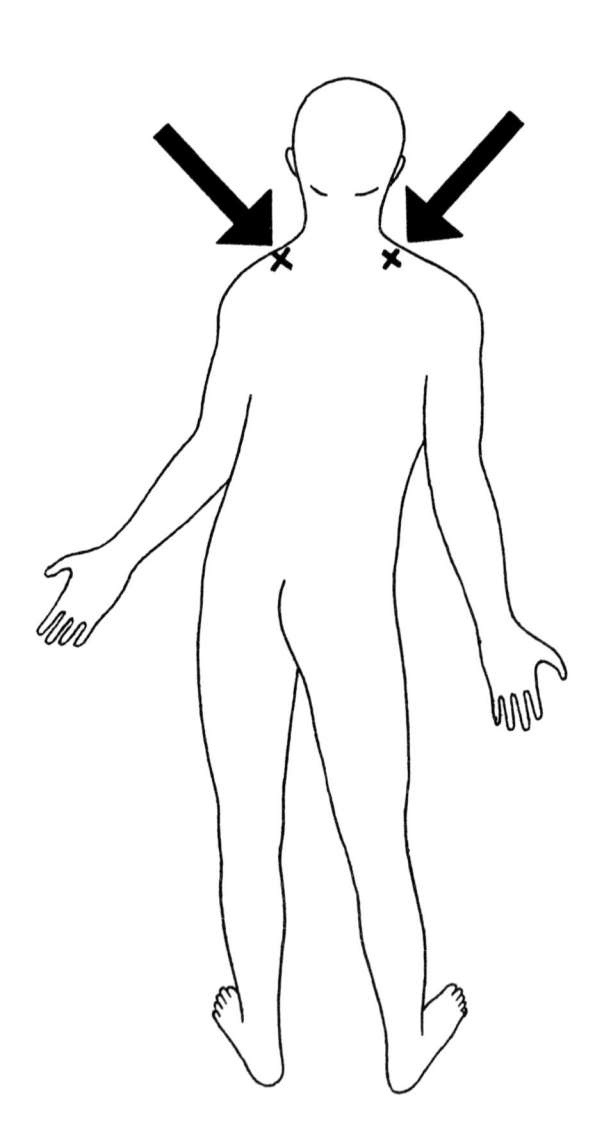

FIGURE 20

▼

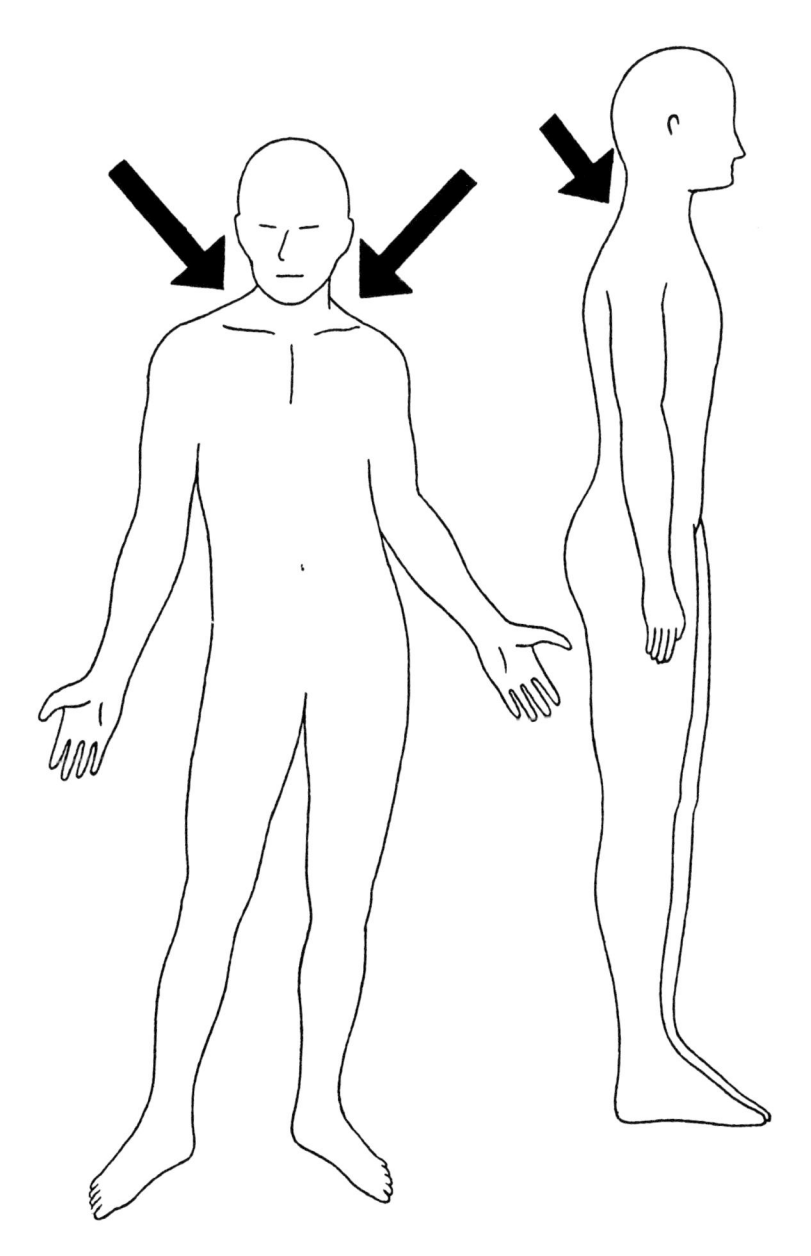

FIGURES 21 AND 22

▼

22   GOUZAO GONGJI   22

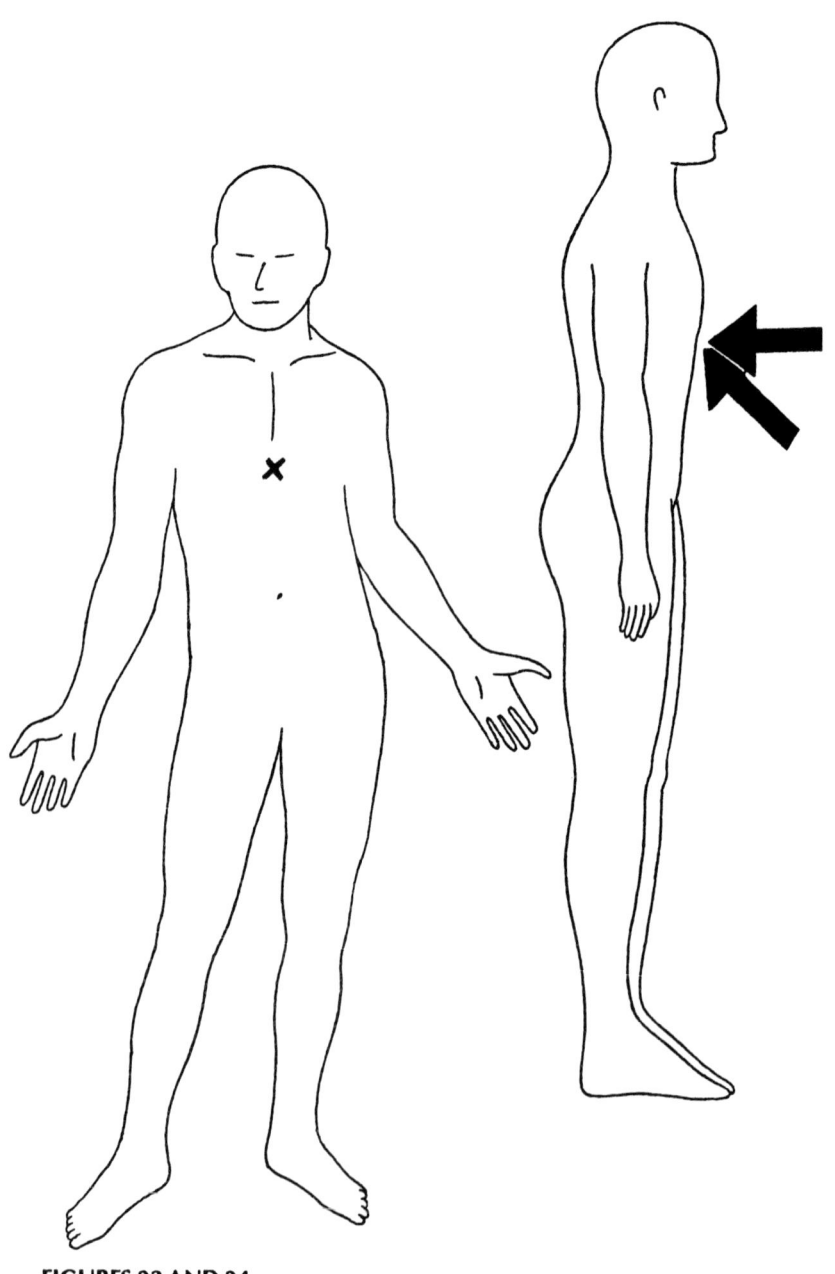

FIGURES 23 AND 24

▼

23 DIRECTIONS OF FORCE 23

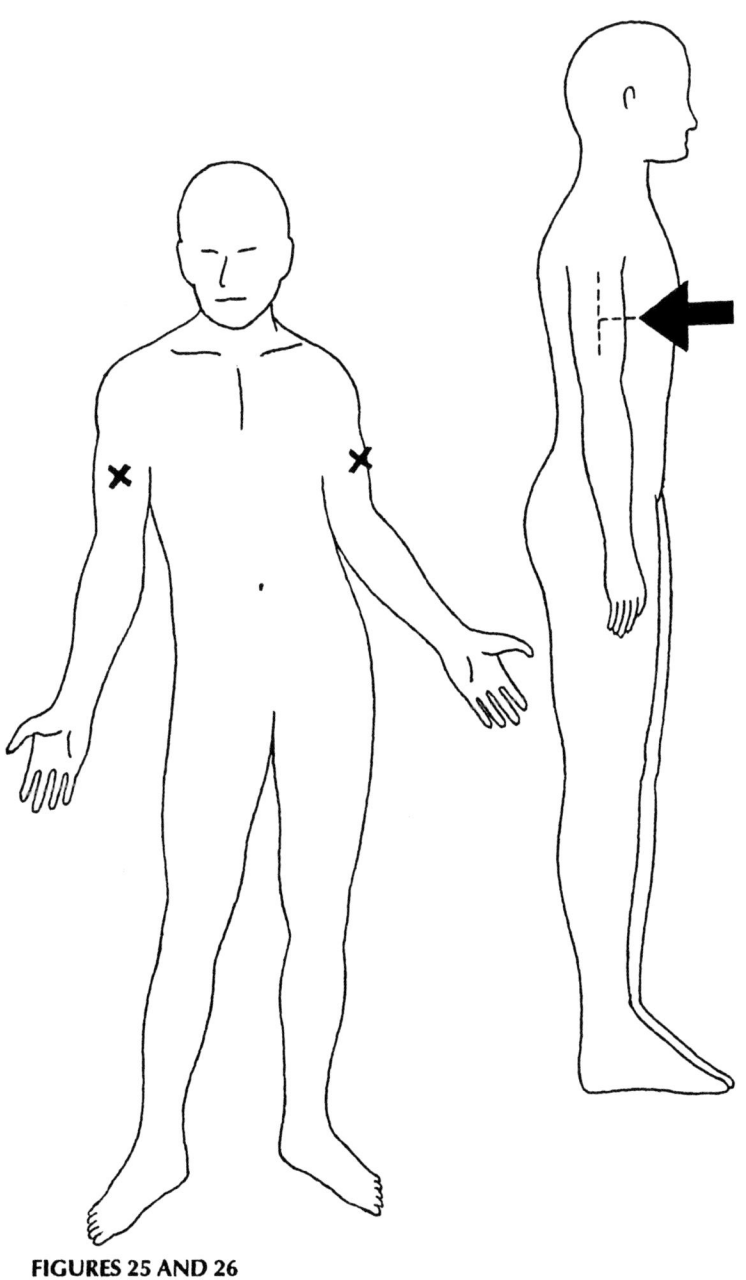

FIGURES 25 AND 26

▼

heel-thrust kick follows the B angle. A slightly downward angle from a punch is also effective against the solar plexus.

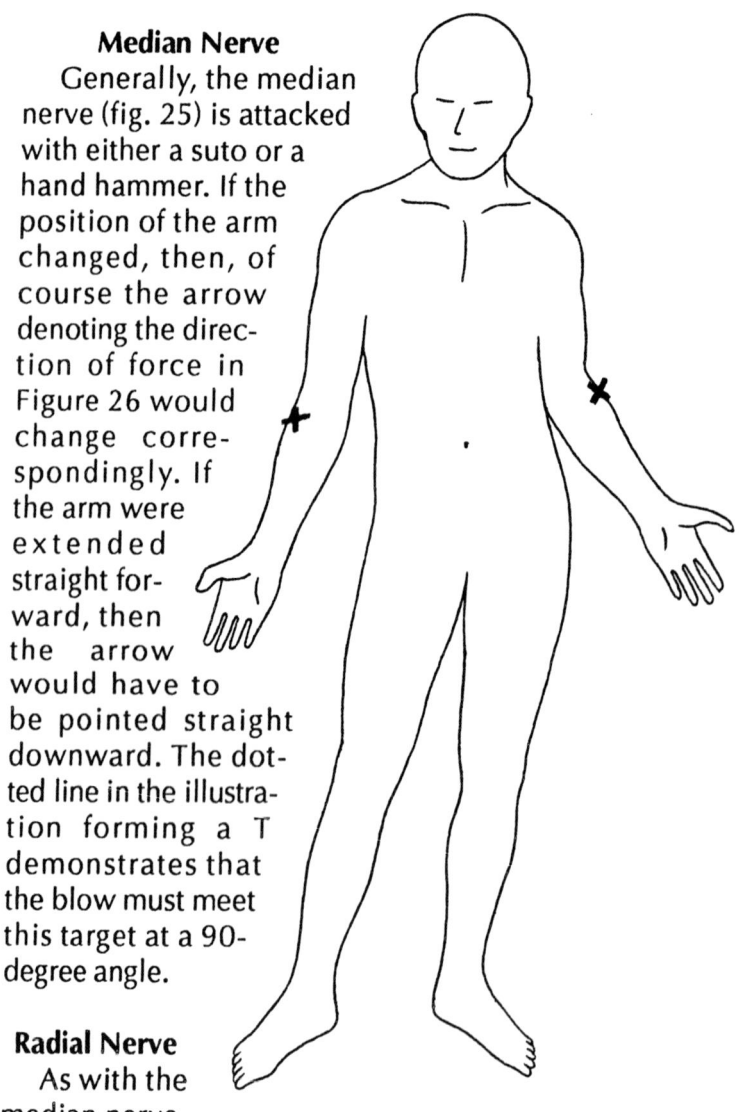

Median Nerve

Generally, the median nerve (fig. 25) is attacked with either a suto or a hand hammer. If the position of the arm changed, then, of course the arrow denoting the direction of force in Figure 26 would change correspondingly. If the arm were extended straight forward, then the arrow would have to be pointed straight downward. The dotted line in the illustration forming a T demonstrates that the blow must meet this target at a 90-degree angle.

Radial Nerve

As with the median nerve, when the tar-

FIGURE 27

get is the radial nerve (fig. 27) the rule of thumb is to attack at a 90-degree angle to the arm. A change in the position of the arm will require a change in the direction of force depicted by the arrows in Figure 28.

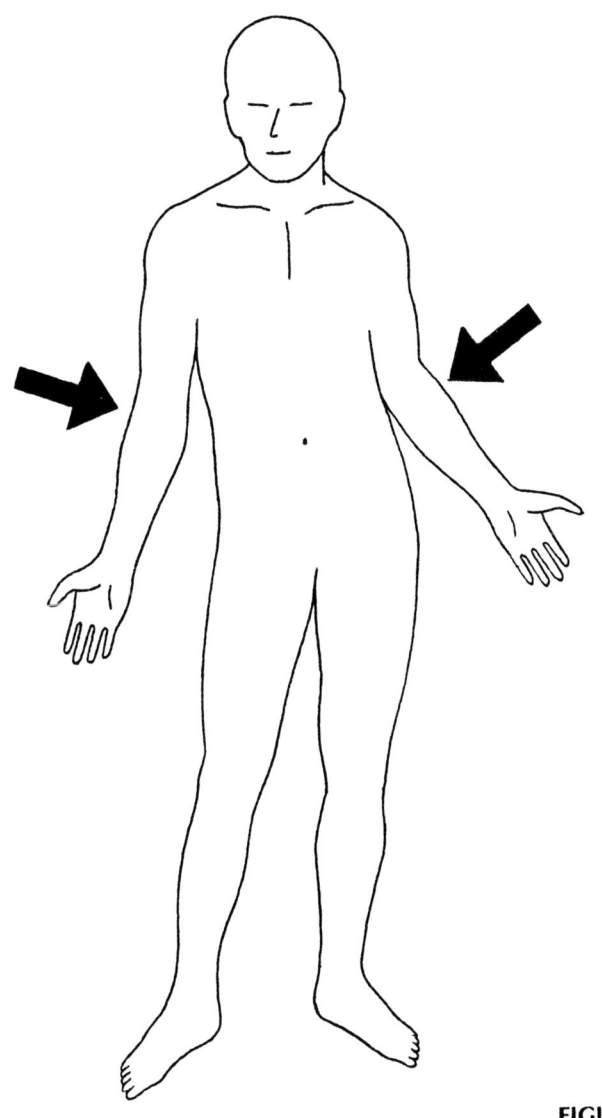

FIGURE 28

▼

CHAPTER THREE

▼ ▼ ▼ ▼ ▼ ▼ ▼ ▼ ▼ ▼ ▼ ▼ ▼

SINGLE-KICK RETURNS

The next four chapters will focus on the practical application of technical movement, using the information from Chapters 1 and 2 as guides to the anatomical targets. As you study these movements, bear in mind that accuracy is crucial. When practicing these techniques, work on the accurate delivery of each block, grapple, and strike, as well as the mechanical execution of the movements.

▼

FIGURE 29

Figures 29 through 32
Figure 29. In this technique you will use an inside suto block and grapple and return a single front kick to the solar plexus. Figure 29 is your starting position.

▼

FIGURE 30

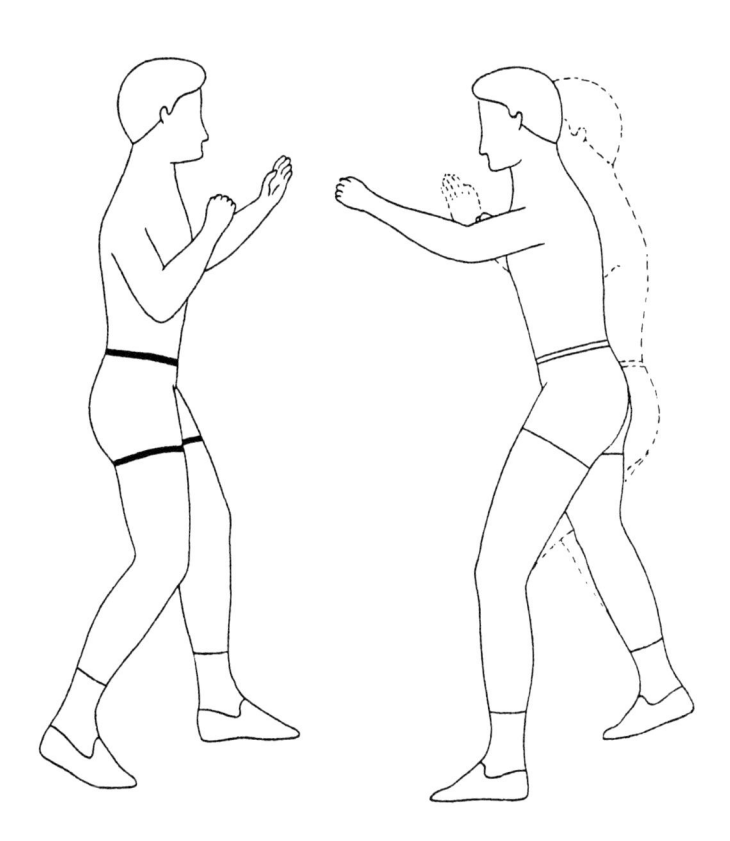

Figure 30. Your opponent has begun a left-handed punch to your upper gate. If the punch is approaching from the outside, an inside crossing block is appropriate.

▼

FIGURE 31

Figure 31. Here you have used an inside suto block while chambering your right leg for a front kick. Note the position of your right hand. The palm was facing across your body before the block; now it is facing your opponent.

▼

FIGURE 32

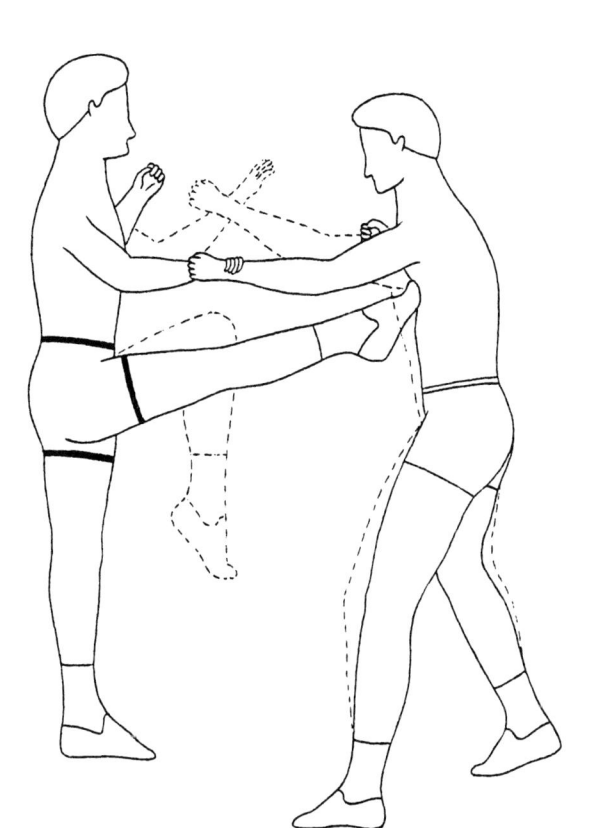

Figure 32. From the block, grapple your opponent's punching arm and extend your chambered kick into his solar plexus.

FIGURE 33

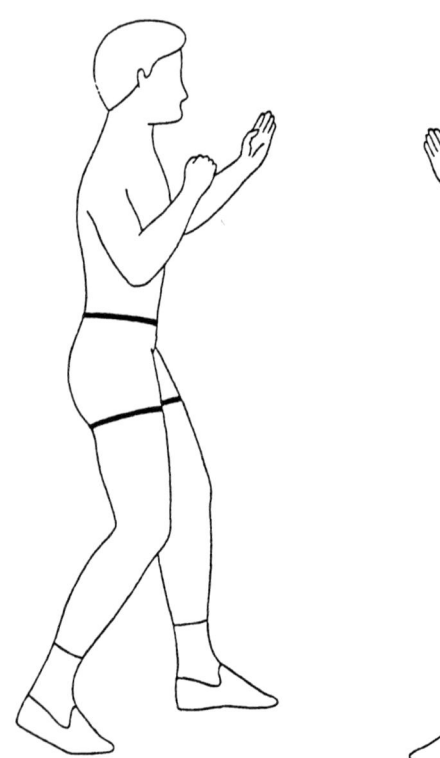

Figures 33 through 36
Figure 33. We will use the inside suto block and grapple again, this time returning a single front kick to the tip of the mandible.

▼

FIGURE 34

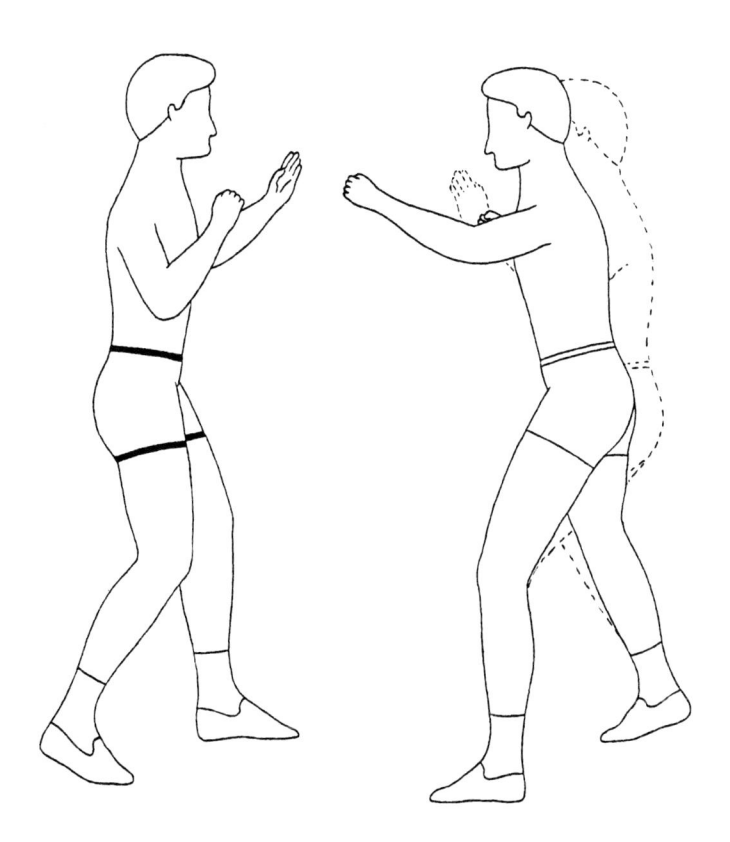

Figure 34. Your opponent has begun a left-handed punch to your upper gate.

▼

FIGURE 35

Figure 35. Here again you have countered the incoming punch with an inside suto block and chambered your right leg for a front kick.

▼

FIGURE 36

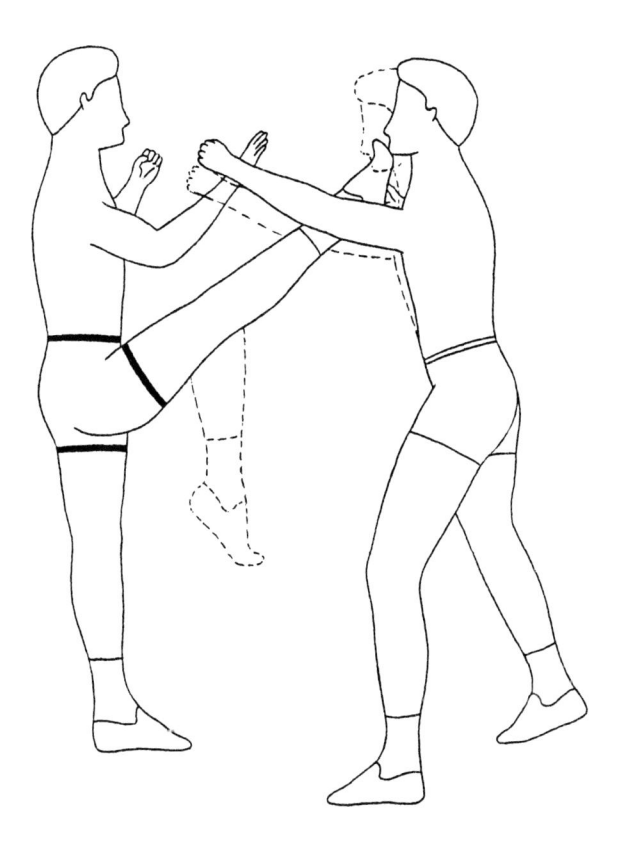

Figure 36. Extend your front kick into your opponent's chin (tip of the mandible). Note that no grapple was used this time. Trapping the arm is optional for single-stroke returns.

▼

FIGURE 37

Figures 37 through 41

Figure 37. We're going to change attacks, defending sides, and kicks in this technique. The starting position remains unchanged, but we will block with the left hand this time and use a kick that will require an adjusting step and a pivot.

▼

FIGURE 38

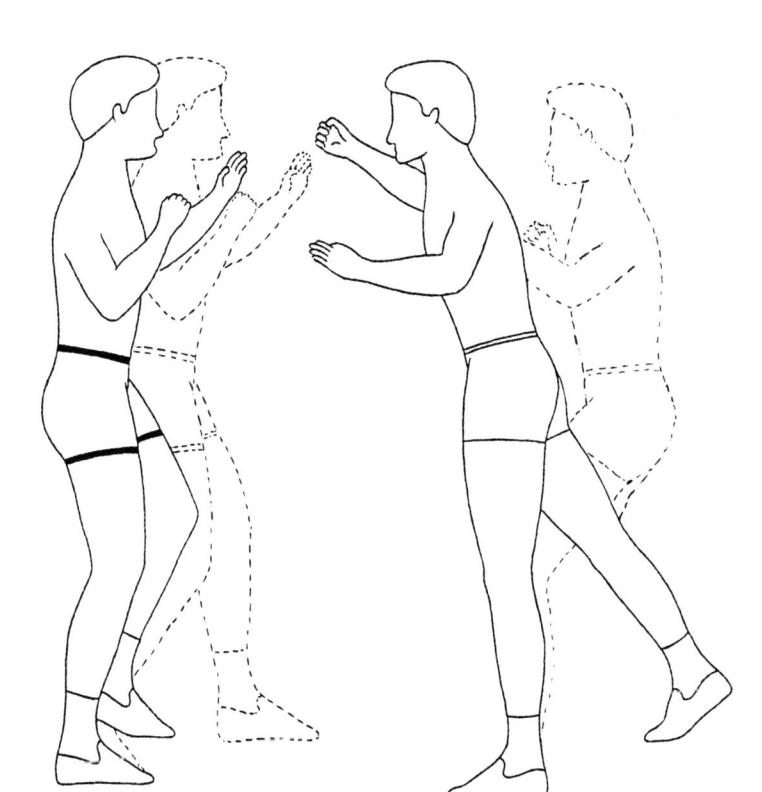

Figure 38. Your opponent has initiated a forward motion, this time approaching with a right-handed punch. Note your adjusting step: the left foot is brought back to the position shown to set the proper distance for the return blow.

▼

FIGURE 39

Figure 39. With the left hand, use an inside suto block to meet and stop the incoming blow. Again, note the direction in which the palm is facing.

▼

FIGURE 40

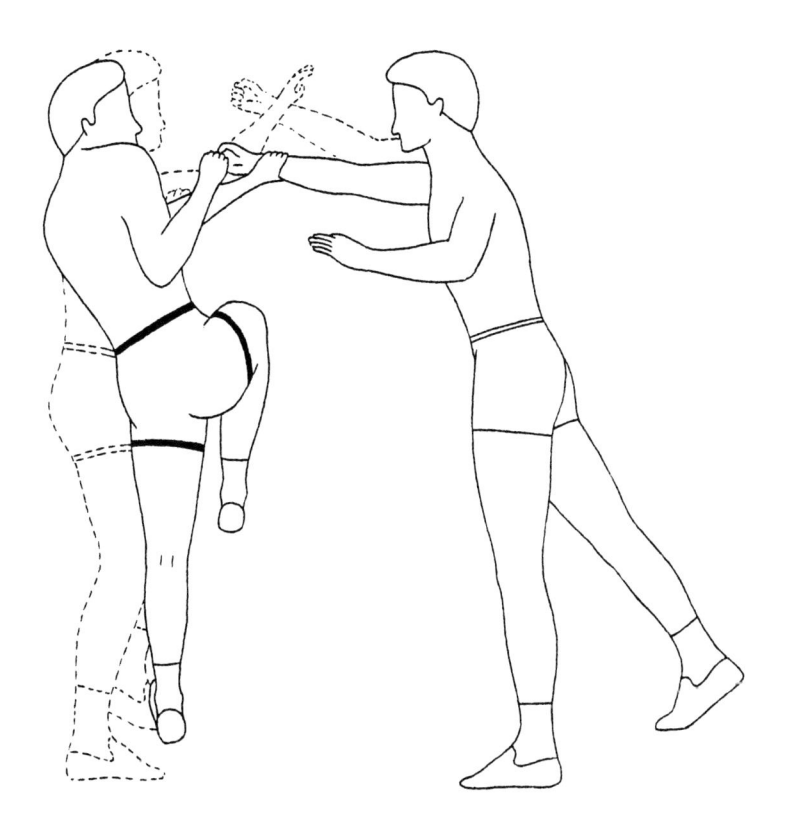

Figure 40. From the block, take a full-handed grip on your opponent's arm at the wrist and rotate your body counterclockwise while chambering a right side kick.

▼

FIGURE 41

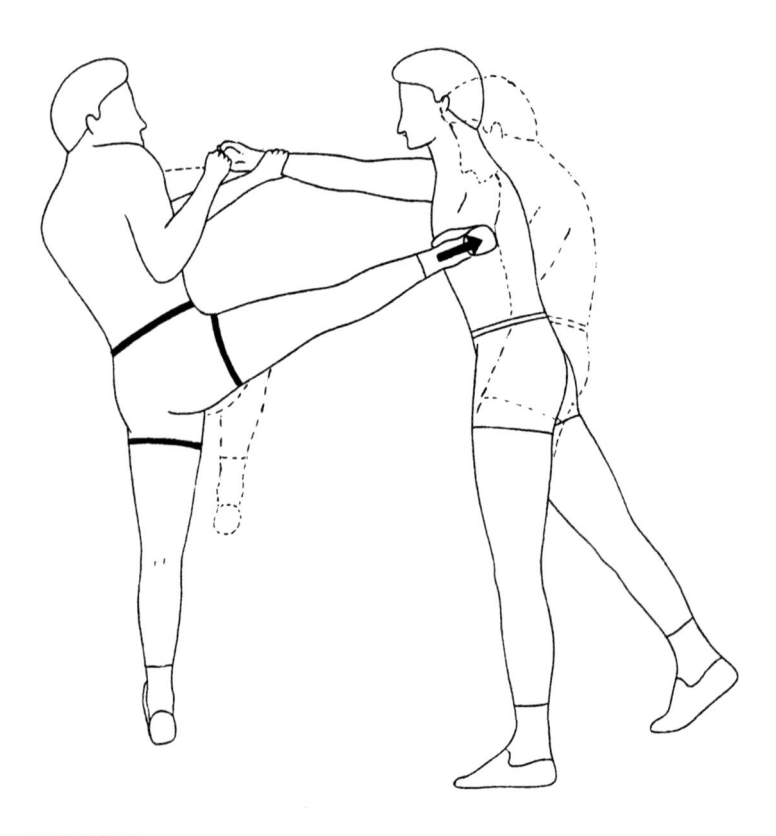

Figure 41. Extend your side kick into your opponent's solar plexus.

FIGURE 42

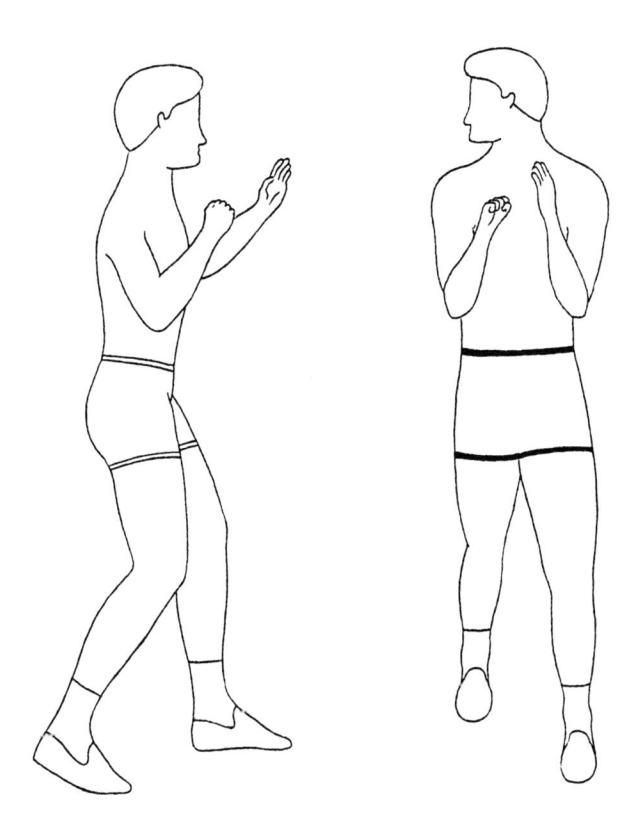

Figures 42 through 45
Figure 42. Note the change in starting positions. Here your opponent is approaching from your east gate. We will use the same kick with the same leg, but note the omission of an adjusting step as the technique progresses.

▼

FIGURE 43

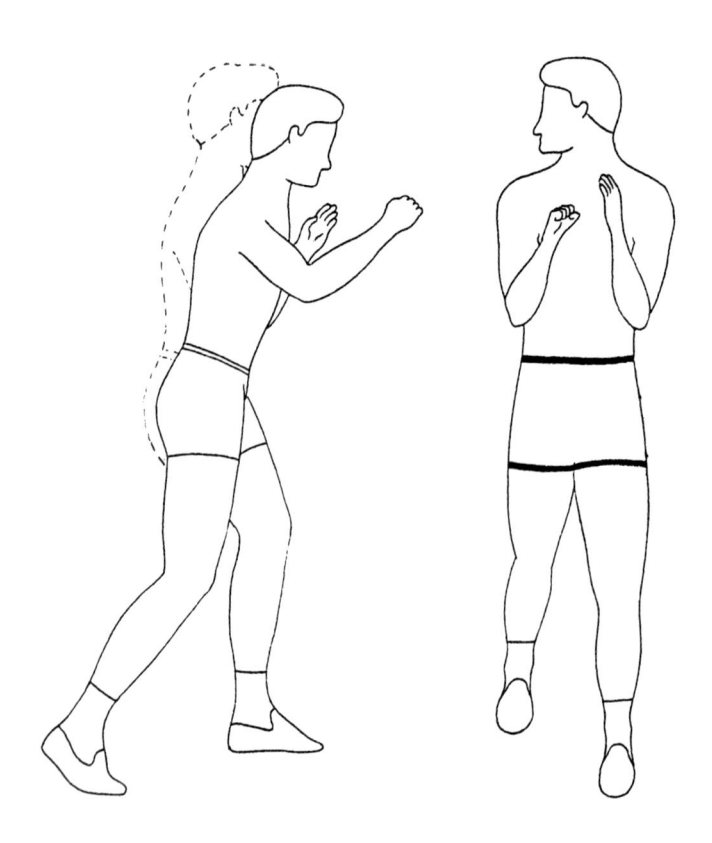

Figure 43. Your opponent has begun his attack using a straight-line punch at your upper gate.

▼

43 SINGLE-KICK RETURNS 43

FIGURE 44

Figure 44. Note the distance between you and your opponent in this illustration. Observe the starting position indicated by the dotted line, as opposed to the solid-line position. By simply shifting your weight onto the foot furthest from your opponent, you increase the gap between the two of you. Because the punch was a straight line, the outside suto block illustrated here is feasible. Your right leg is chambered for a side kick as you block.

▼

FIGURE 45

Figure 45. Extend your side kick into your opponent's solar plexus while grappling his punching arm.

FIGURE 46

Figures 46 through 50

Figure 46. You are positioned with your opponent at your north gate. You'll use the side kick once again, but you will change targets.

▼

FIGURE 47

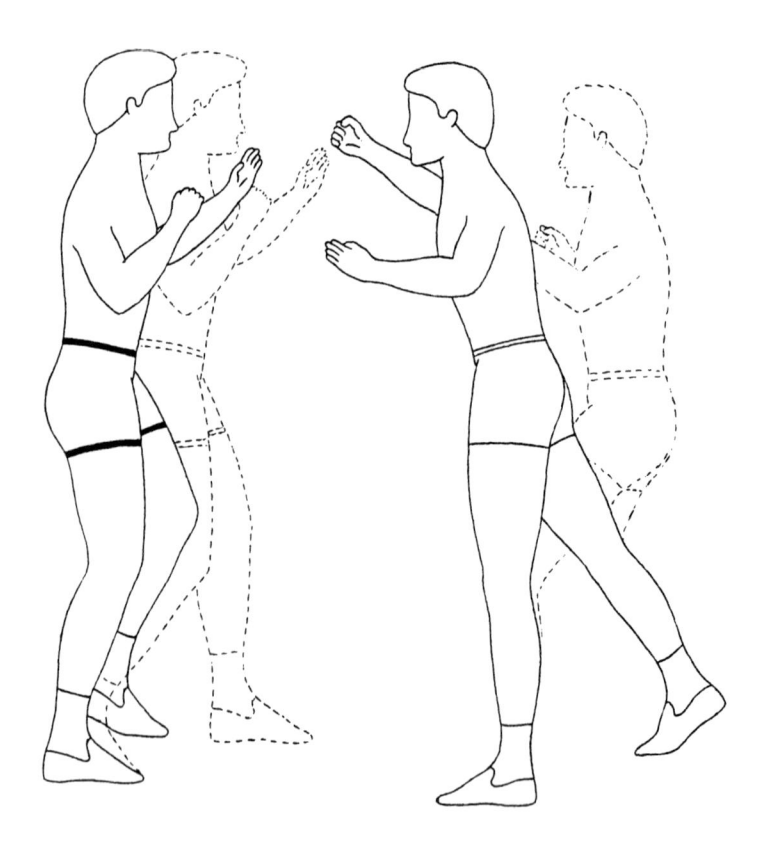

Figure 47. Your opponent has started an advance with a high right-hand punch. Note that he is not taking an advancing step. He is closing the gap by shifting his weight onto his front leg.

▼

FIGURE 48

Figure 48. Using a left suto block, stop the incoming punch at the wrist. Note the rotation of the palm on the blocking hand.

▼

FIGURE 49

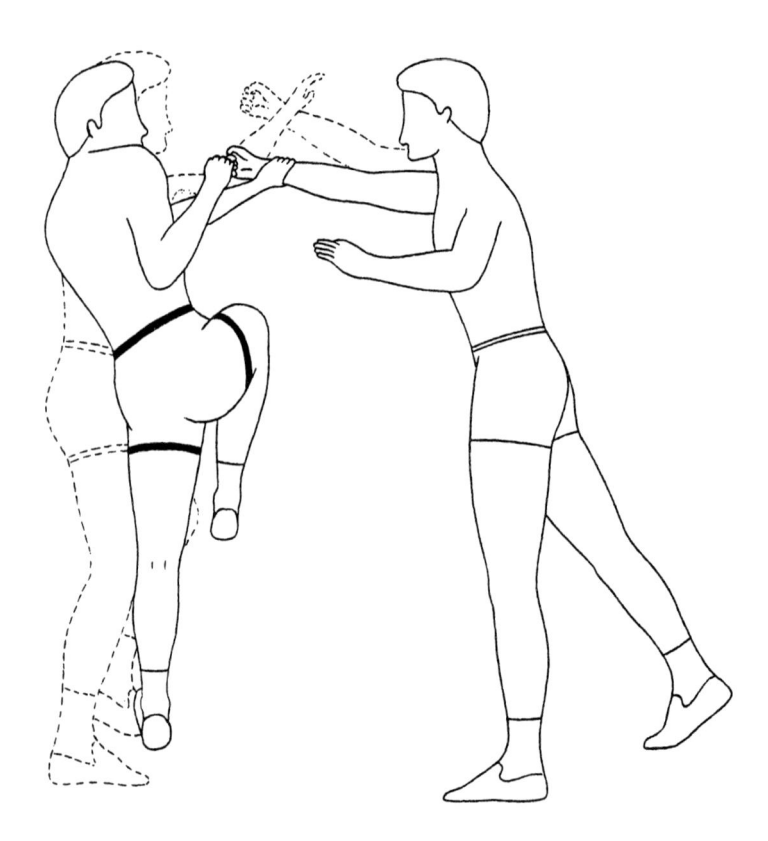

Figure 49. Take a full grip of your opponent's arm while shifting your weight onto the left leg. Rotate your body as illustrated and chamber your right leg for a side kick.

FIGURE 50

Figure 50. Lock your side kick out, striking your opponent on the tip of the mandible.

▼

FIGURE 51

Figures 51 through 55

Figure 51. With your opponent positioned at your north gate, you will use the same block and adjusting step as in the previous set, but this time you'll use a different kick.

▼

FIGURE 52

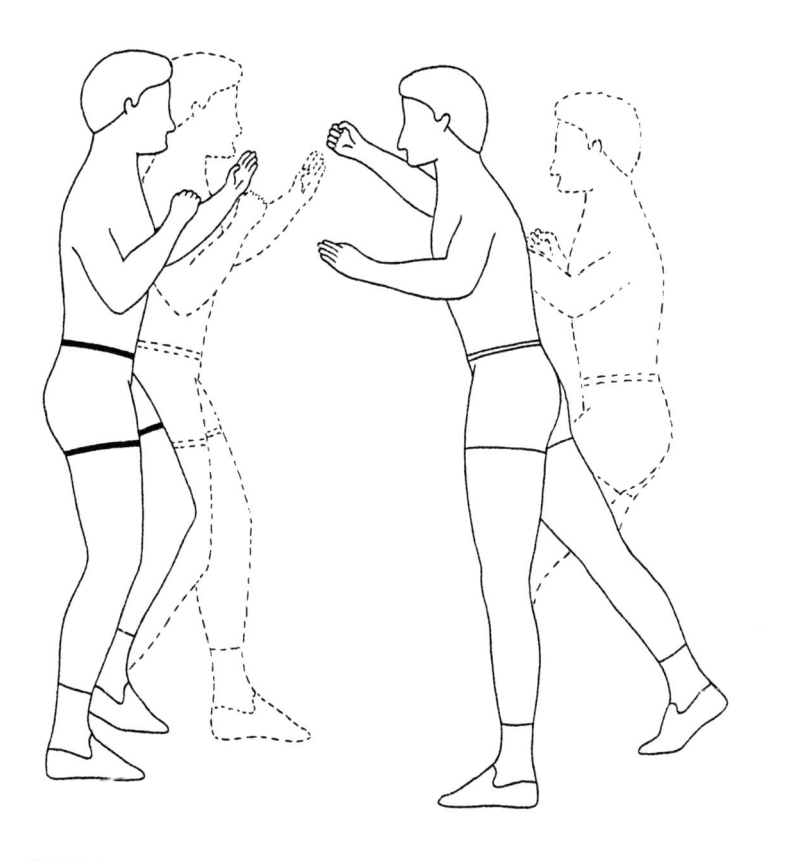

Figure 52. Your opponent advances with a high-gate right roundhouse punch.

▼

FIGURE 53

Figure 53. With your distance properly adjusted by the step depicted in Figure 52, stop the incoming blow with an inside suto block.

▼

FIGURE 54

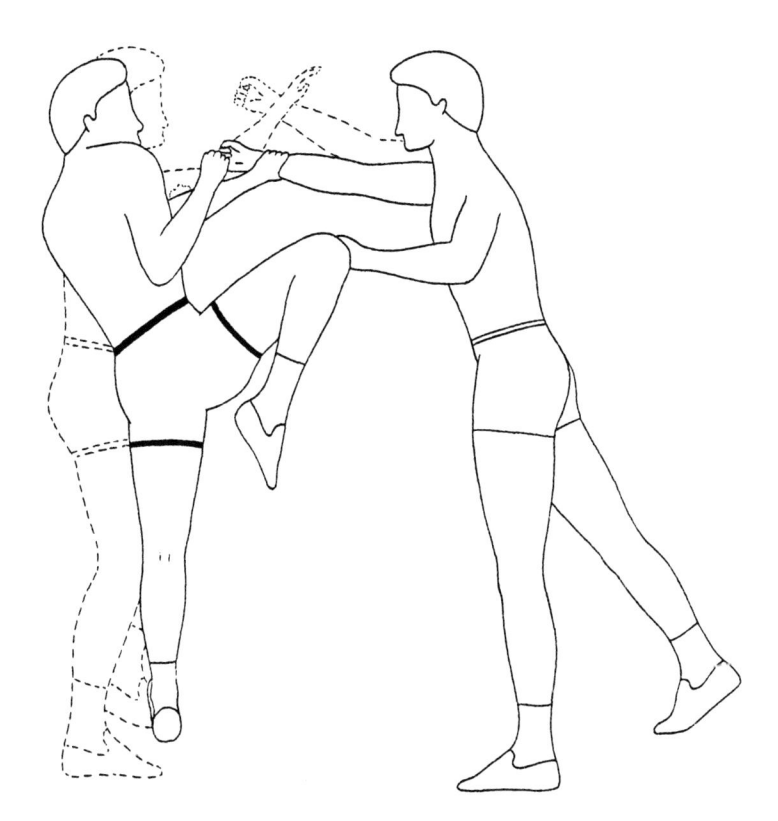

Figure 54. Take a full grip on the arm with the blocking hand, shift and rotate your body on the left leg, and chamber your right leg for a roundhouse kick. Note the difference in this kick chamber position as opposed to that depicted in Figure 49.

▼

FIGURE 55

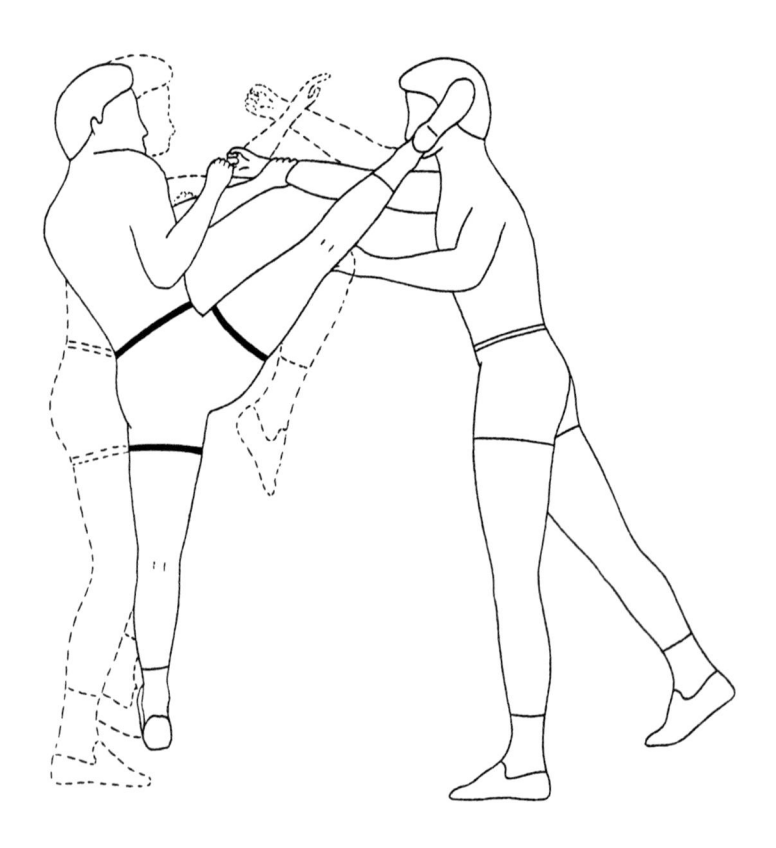

Figure 55. Extend your roundhouse kick into your opponent's ear.

FIGURE 56

Figures 56 through 58

Figure 56. We are going to completely change our defensive mechanics for these last two techniques. So far we've used blocks, adjusting steps, rotations, and the front, side, and roundhouse kicks. In these two techniques we will eliminate blocks and adjusting steps and use a different kick. As depicted in the illustration, the opponent is at the north gate.

▼

FIGURE 57

Figure 57. Your opponent advances with a straight-line half-turn punch with his left hand. Chamber your right leg for a heel-thrust kick as he begins his approach.

FIGURE 58

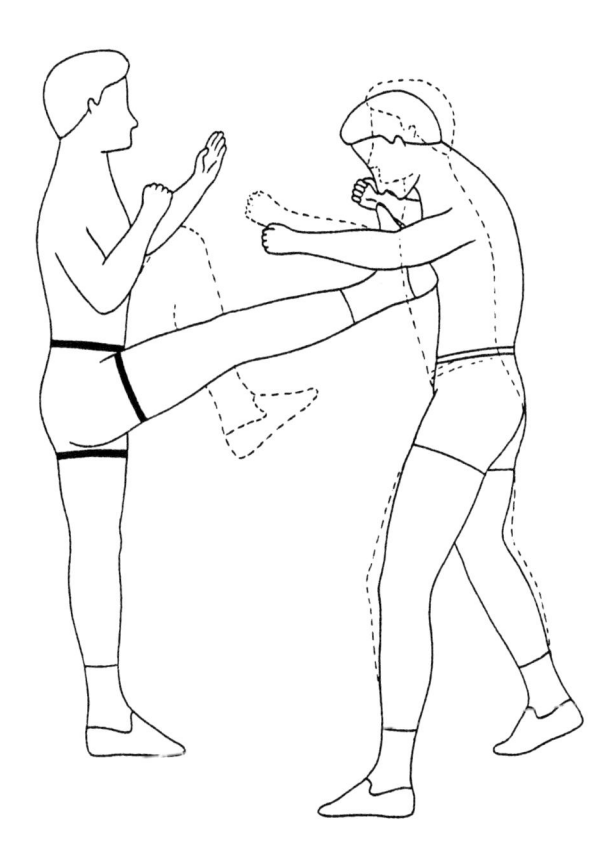

Figure 58. Lock your heel-thrust kick out into your opponent's solar plexus.

▼

FIGURE 59

Figures 59 through 61

Figure 59. Again you start with your opponent at your north gate. You'll use the same chamber position and kick, but against a different target.

FIGURE 60

Figure 60. As your opponent approaches with his left-handed punch, chamber your heel-thrust kick on the right side. Note the difference between this chamber position and those of the front, side, and roundhouse kicks discussed earlier in the chapter.

▼

FIGURE 61

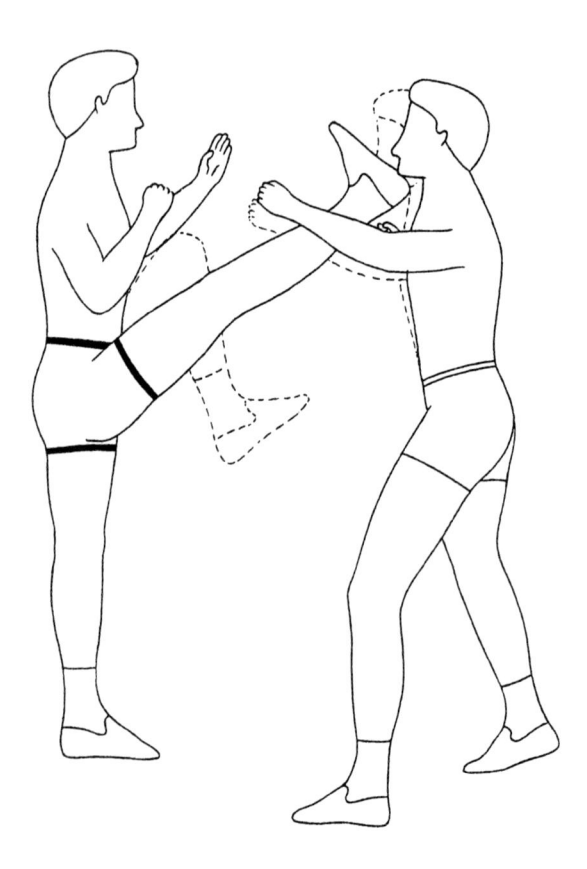

Figure 61. Extend your heel-thrust kick out high into the tip of your opponent's mandible.

CHAPTER FOUR

SINGLE-PUNCH RETURNS

Along with the accurate delivery of return strikes, flow must be incorporated into your movements. Choppy, sluggish delivery of return strikes causes them to be slower and, consequently, less effective and less likely to land. Constant repetition of techniques, if practiced with concentrated effort, will smooth out the movements, enhancing their efficiency. Knowledge is gained through study; skill is gained through practice.

▼

FIGURE 62

Figures 62 through 65
Figure 62. By this time you should be familiar with the inside suto block. We will use that and one additional block in this chapter. Your starting position is facing your opponent.

FIGURE 63

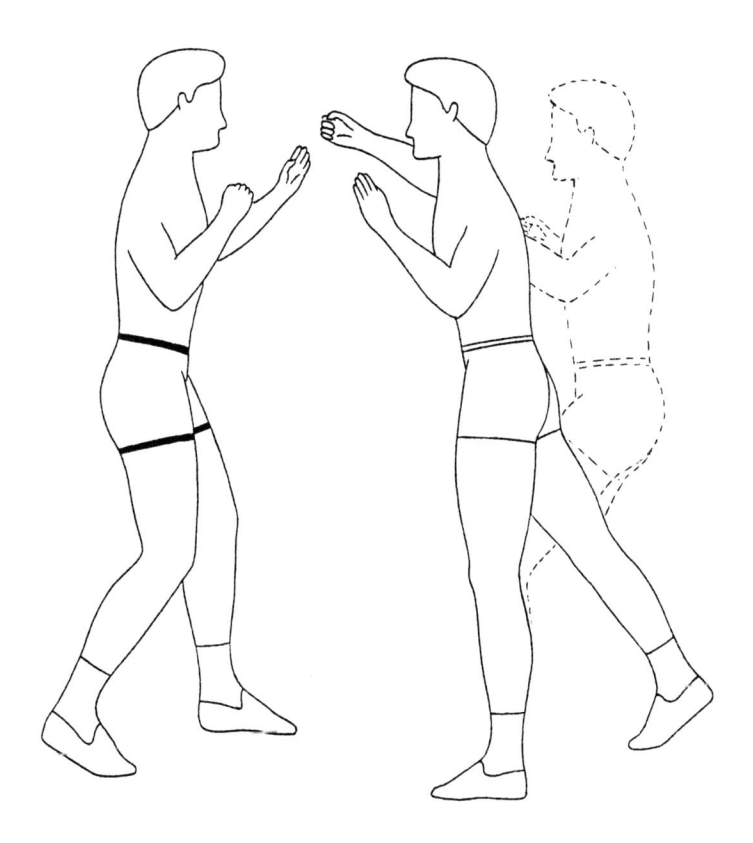

Figure 63. Your opponent advances with a wide, high right-hand punch. Note again that he does not step, but merely leans toward you to get into punching range.

▼

FIGURE 64

Figure 64. Stop the incoming blow with an inside suto block, and change your right-hand chamber position from mid-range to a high suto chamber position.

FIGURE 65

Figure 65. Extend your right arm in an arc while forming a cup with your hand, and strike the opponent on his left ear.

▼

FIGURE 66

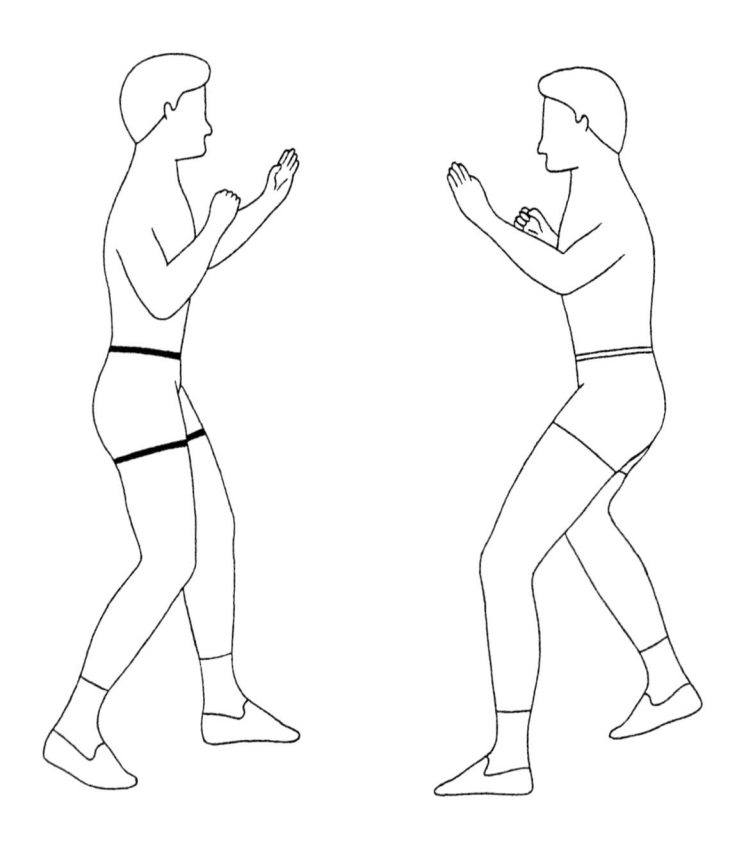

Figures 66 through 69
Figure 66. Starting from the facing position, we will use essentially the same strike, but we will use two hands simultaneously instead of one.

▼

FIGURE 67

Figure 67. Your opponent approaches with a high, wide right-handed punch and with a lean, not a step.

▼

FIGURE 68

Figure 68. Use the same block and chamber position you used in the previous sequence.

FIGURE 69

Figure 69. Forming both hands into shallow cups, slap both of your opponent's ears simultaneously.

FIGURE 70

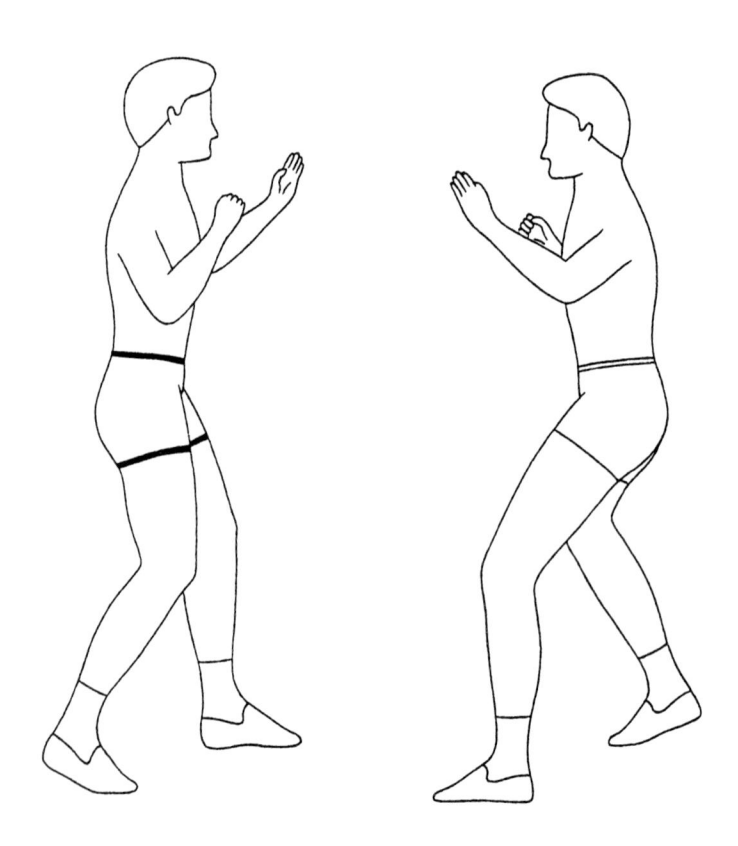

Figures 70 through 73

Figure 70. In this technique you're going to block the same punch with the same movement we used in the previous sequence, and you'll rechamber the right hand to the high suto position again, but you'll seek a different target with your return strike.

▼

71 SINGLE-PUNCH RETURNS 71

FIGURE 71

Figure 71. Your opponent approaches with a wide, high right-handed punch.

▼

FIGURE 72

Figure 72. Stop the incoming blow with an inside suto block while simultaneously repositioning your right hand into a high suto chamber position.

FIGURE 73

Figure 73. Grapple your opponent's right arm and deliver a downward, vertical suto to his brachial plexus. (Refer to *Iron Hand of the Dragon's Touch* for the precise contact point of the suto weapon.)

▼

FIGURE 74

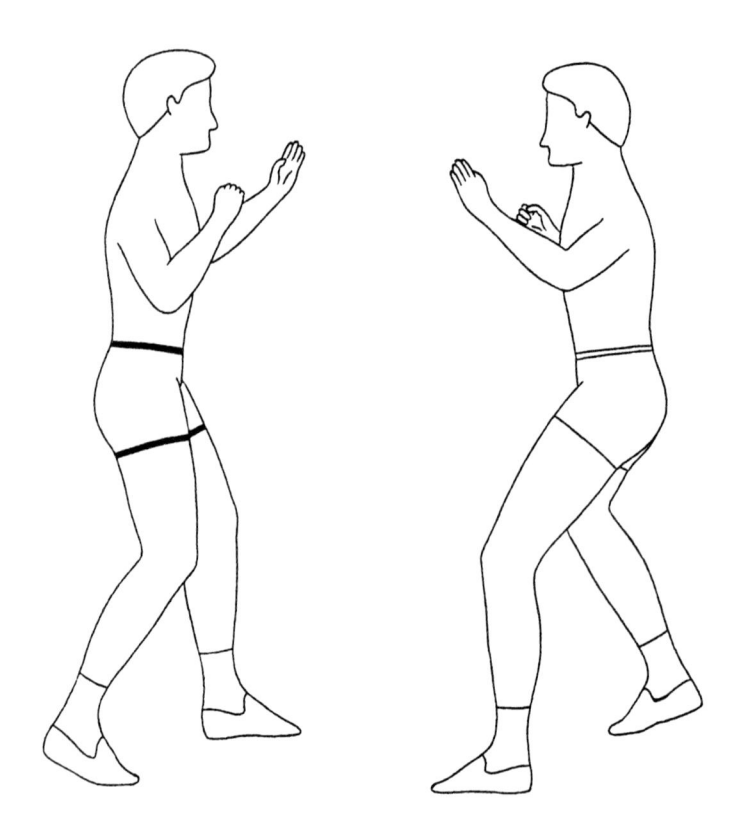

Figures 74 through 77

Figure 74. In this technique we're going to change blocks and use a closed-hand return. The contact point of the block is on the underside of the arm from the heel of the hand to approximately three inches above the fold of the wrist.

▼

FIGURE 75

Figure 75. Your opponent begins an advance: his attack is a right-handed punch following a straight line to the end of the upper gate.

▼

FIGURE 76

Figure 76. Mimicking a scooping motion, deflect the incoming blow just outside the width of your body. Note the position of the elbow of the blocking arm.

▼

FIGURE 77

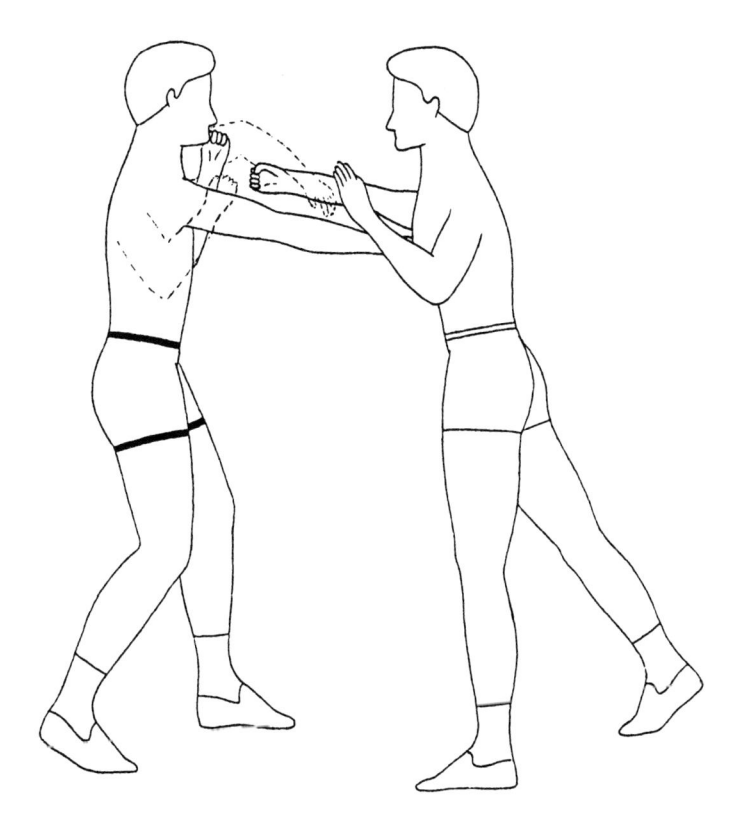

Figure 77. While returning the blocking arm to the high-punch chamber position, extend a right half-turn punch to your opponent's solar plexus.

▼

FIGURE 78

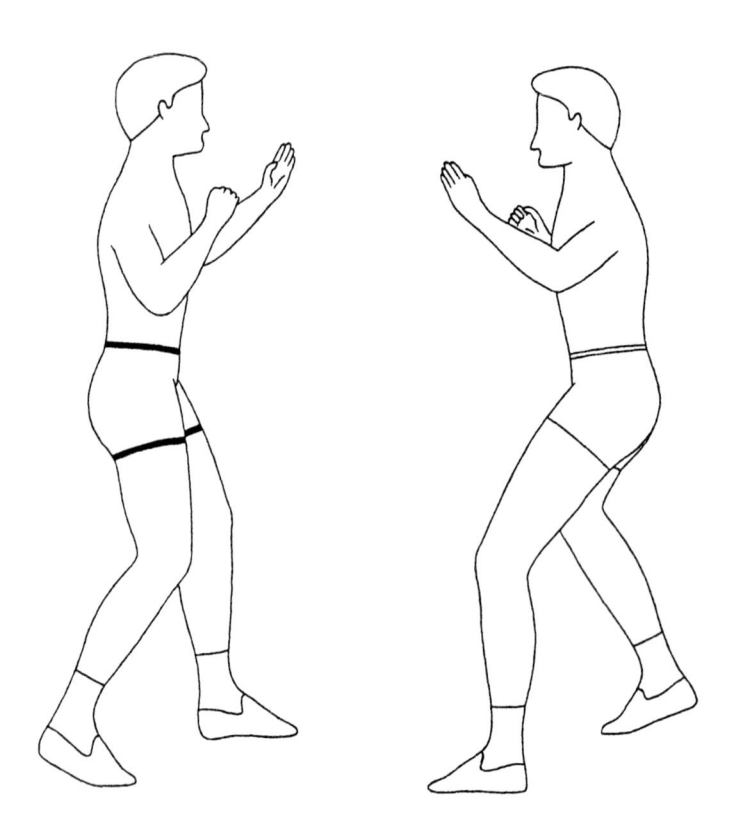

Figures 78 through 81

Figure 78. The scooping palm block may be used to defend against high upper- as well as lower-gate punches. You simply raise the blocking arm to the height corresponding to the incoming punch, bringing the offending arm down and outside the width of the body.

▼

FIGURE 79

Figure 79. Your opponent initiates the high-gate punch. Note again that he does not take a step; he closes the gap and brings himself within striking range by shifting his body weight onto his left leg.

▼

FIGURE 80

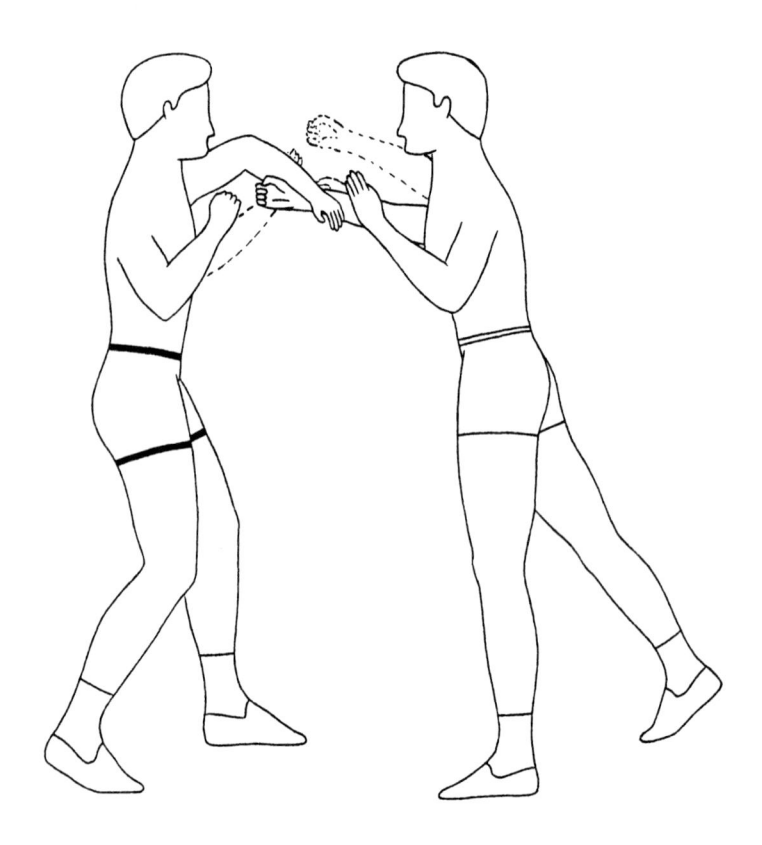

Figure 80. Raise your blocking arm to the necessary height and redirect the incoming blow down and to the outside of the width of your body.

FIGURE 81

Figure 81. While chambering the blocking arm, snap out a straight-line half-turn punch to the tip of your opponent's mandible.

For the remainder of this chapter we will focus on two pressure points: the median nerve and the radial nerve. Because these targets do not occupy a central position in the body or affect a major organ, they are often disregarded as ineffective pressure points. The contrary is true. As we learned in *Guge Gongji*, damaging an appendage neutralizes the corresponding quarter of the body. While the pressure points targeted in *Guge Gongji* affected an entirely different anatomical system, targeting the median and radial nerves has very similar results.

FIGURE 82

Figures 82 through 85

Figure 82. By this time you are familiar with the block and high suto chamber positions used in this sequence. It is especially important to hold the wrist firmly in this technique to stabilize the target.

▼

FIGURE 83

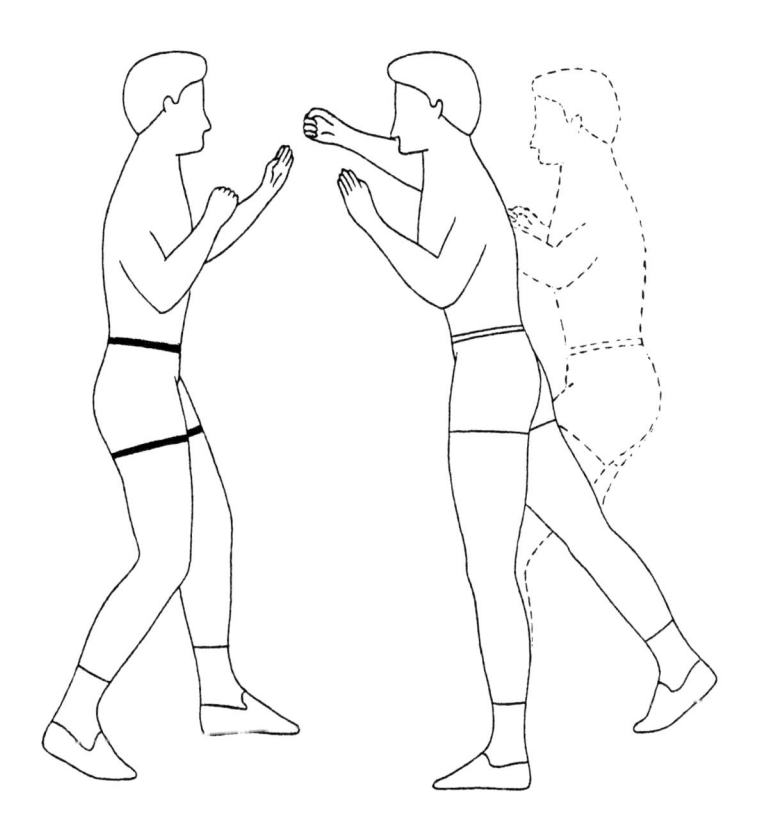

Figure 83. This is a high roundhouse punch aimed at your upper gate.

▼

FIGURE 84

Figure 84. Stop the incoming blow with a left inside suto block, while chambering the right hand at the high suto position.

FIGURE 85

Figure 85. Lower your blocking hand and tightly grab your opponent's arm at the wrist. Bring your suto down across your body, striking the median nerve of the offending arm.

▼

FIGURE 86

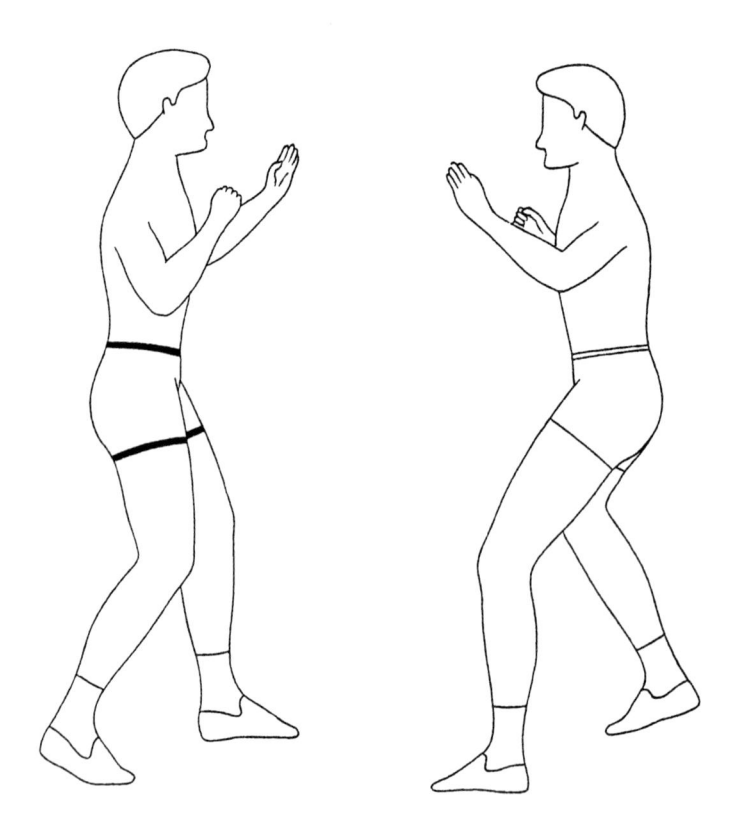

Figures 86 through 89

Figure 86. Starting from the same position, your block, grapple, and rechamber of the return weapon will be the same, but you'll alter the position of the striking hand.

▼

FIGURE 87

Figure 87. The opponent initiates his offensive move, approaching with a wide right-hand punch aimed at your high gate.

▼

FIGURE 88

Figure 88. Stop the incoming blow with a left inside suto block while chambering the right hand at the high suto position.

▼

FIGURE 89

Figure 89. Clamp the offending arm tightly at the wrist, and bring a hammer strike down into your opponent's median nerve.

▼

FIGURE 90

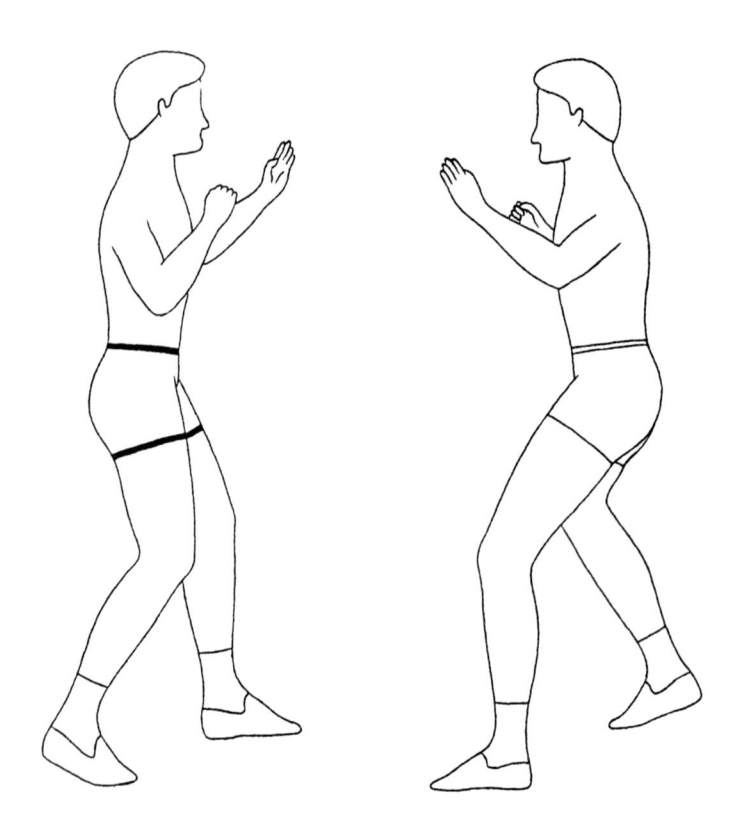

Figures 90 through 93

Figure 90. We will strike the radial nerve in the next two techniques. Note the close proximity of this target to the median nerve. On the average man's arm, the radial and median nerves are within six inches of each other, both being distal branches of the brachial plexus.

FIGURE 91

Figure 91. The incoming punch is again a high right roundhouse punch to the upper gate.

▼

FIGURE 92

Figure 92. Stop the incoming blow with an inside suto block while simultaneously repositioning your right hand to the suto chamber position.

FIGURE 93

Figure 93. Grasping the offending arm tightly to stabilize it, bring your right suto down into the opponent's radial nerve.

FIGURE 94

Figures 94 through 96

In this final technique for Chapter 4, you will again seek the radial nerve as a target, but you will use a hand hammer strike.

Figure 94. The attack is a wide right roundhouse punch aimed at your upper vertical gate.

▼

FIGURE 95

Figure 95. Stop the incoming blow with an inside suto block while simultaneously changing the position of the right hand to the high suto chamber position.

FIGURE 96

Figure 96. Rotate the blocking hand and tightly hold the opponent's wrist to stabilize the arm. Bring your hand hammer down into your opponent's radial nerve.

CHAPTER FIVE

COMBINATION KICKS

For combinations to be effective, the movements must go beyond familiarity and application of the primary elements. Combinations must be characterized by fluidity from the very first movement through the impact of the final blow and the return to the starting position. The time between the first and second strikes must be minimized, and the effort toward achieving speed and flow mandates a watchful eye over the opponent. A blocked or avoided first strike may necessitate aborting the combination midway through its progress to avoid or counter a vulnerable body position. Good combinations can be difficult to block, but they must be honed through repeated practice if their full combative potential is to be realized.

FIGURE 97

Figures 97 through 102

Figure 97. In this sequence, we will use the same kick two times, striking one low and one high anatomical target out of those we're focusing on in this study. Chamber positions, especially for second strikes, are crucial elements in combinations. Often, practitioners will shorten one or both of the strikes in a combination too much in an attempt to increase the speed of the delivery. With some combinations a shortened stroke is acceptable because a change in the direction of force from one strike to the other leaves a sufficient distance from which to generate momentum. All of the combinations in this and the following chapter will be illustrated with full chamber positions.

▼

FIGURE 98

Figure 98. Your opponent begins a forward shift while initiating a left straight-line punch to your high gate.

FIGURE 99

Figure 99. Deflect the incoming blow with an inside suto block, shift your weight and balance onto your left leg, and chamber your right leg for a front kick.

▼

FIGURE 100

Figure 100. Rotating your palm clockwise, grapple your opponent's arm at the wrist and extend your front kick into his solar plexus.

▼

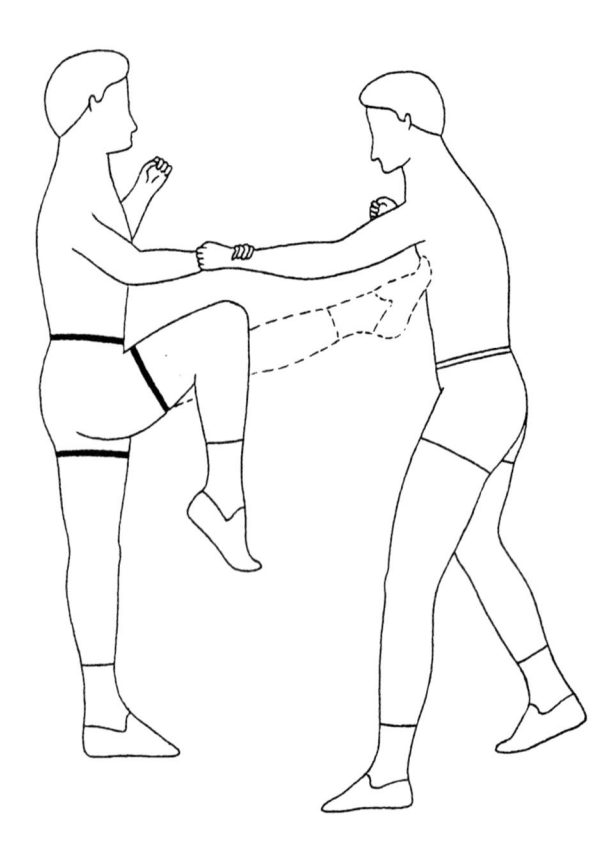

FIGURE 101

Figure 101. Retain the grip on the offending arm and rechamber your right leg for another front kick.

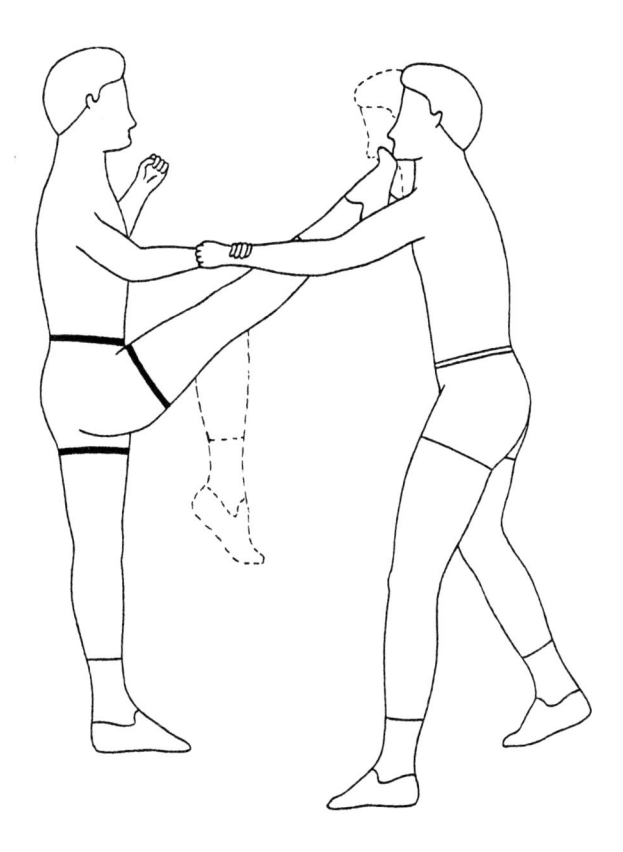

FIGURE 102

Figure 102. For your final stroke, extend your front kick into the tip of your opponent's mandible while retaining your grip on his wrist.

▼

FIGURE 103

Figures 103 through 108

Figure 103. This sequence will be a bit more complicated than the first. Because we will be using two kicks requiring different chamber positions and different directions of force, a second shift in body weight and a rotation will be required to complete the combination.

▼

FIGURE 104

Figure 104. Your opponent has begun a forward shift while initiating a left straight-line punch to your upper gate.

▼

FIGURE 105

Figure 105. Deflect the incoming blow with an inside suto block, shift your weight and balance onto your left leg, and chamber your right leg for a front kick.

▼

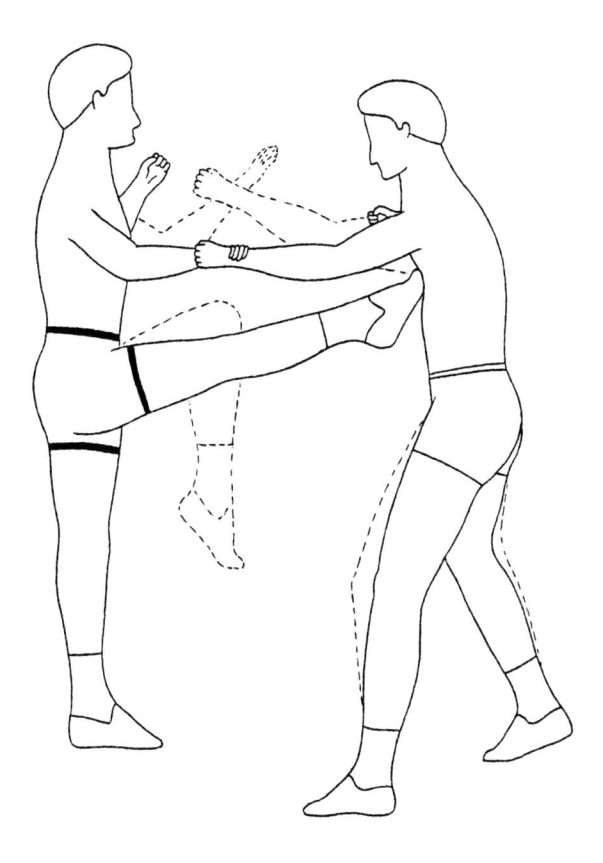

FIGURE 106

Figure 106. Rotating your palm clockwise, grapple your opponent's arm at the wrist and extend your front kick into his solar plexus.

▼

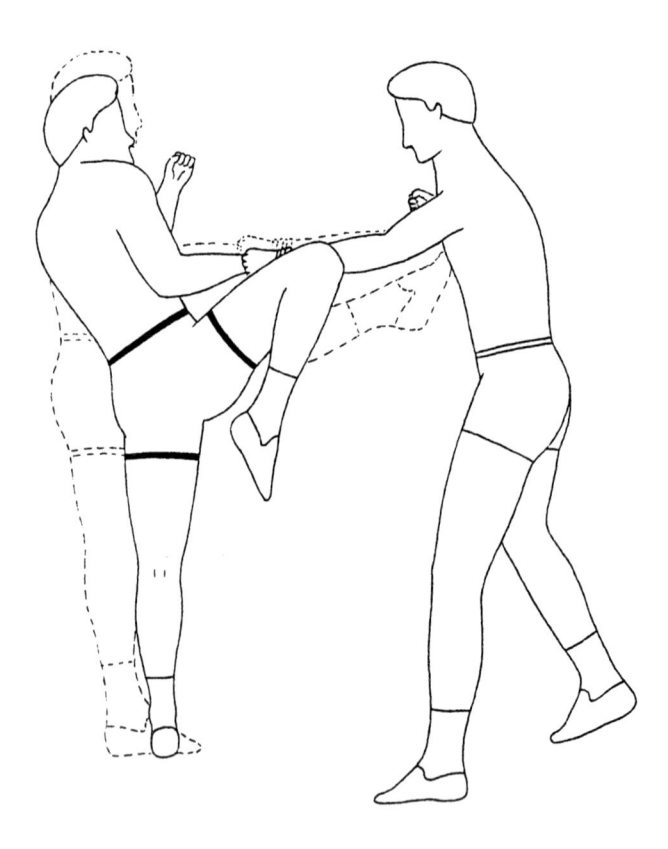

FIGURE 107

Figure 107. Observe this chamber position as opposed to the one in Figure 105. This chamber position is for a high roundhouse kick. Note that the opponent's offending arm has been brought to the inside and that the knee of the kicking leg is now positioned to the outside of that arm.

▼

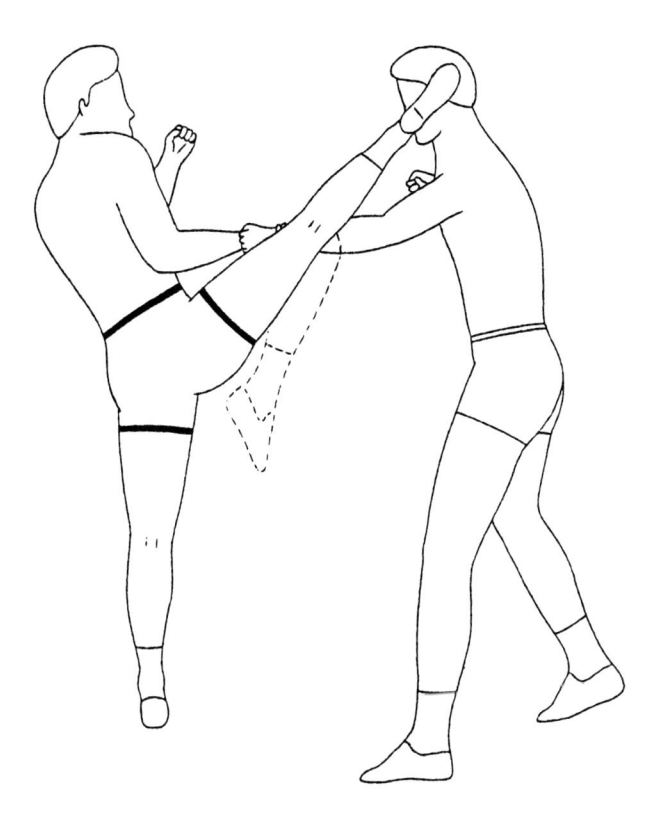

FIGURE 108

Figure 108. Extend your roundhouse kick to your opponent's ear.

▼

FIGURE 109

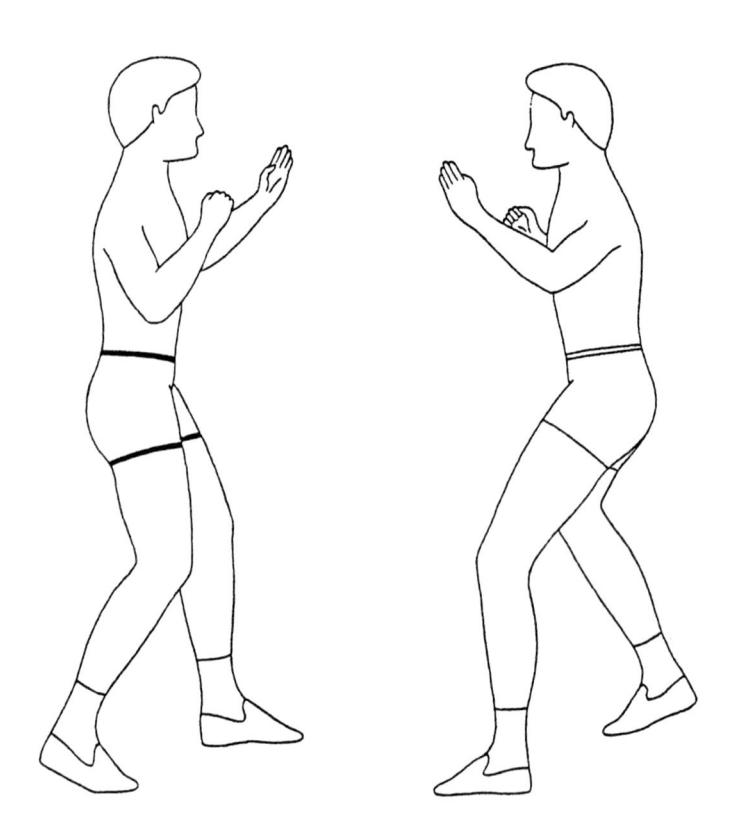

Figures 109 through 115

Figure 109. As we learned in Chapter 3, because of the varying lengths of the different kicks, an adjusting step is sometimes required. In this combination, we will lead with a side kick, which, at this proximity, requires just such a range-adjusting step.

▼

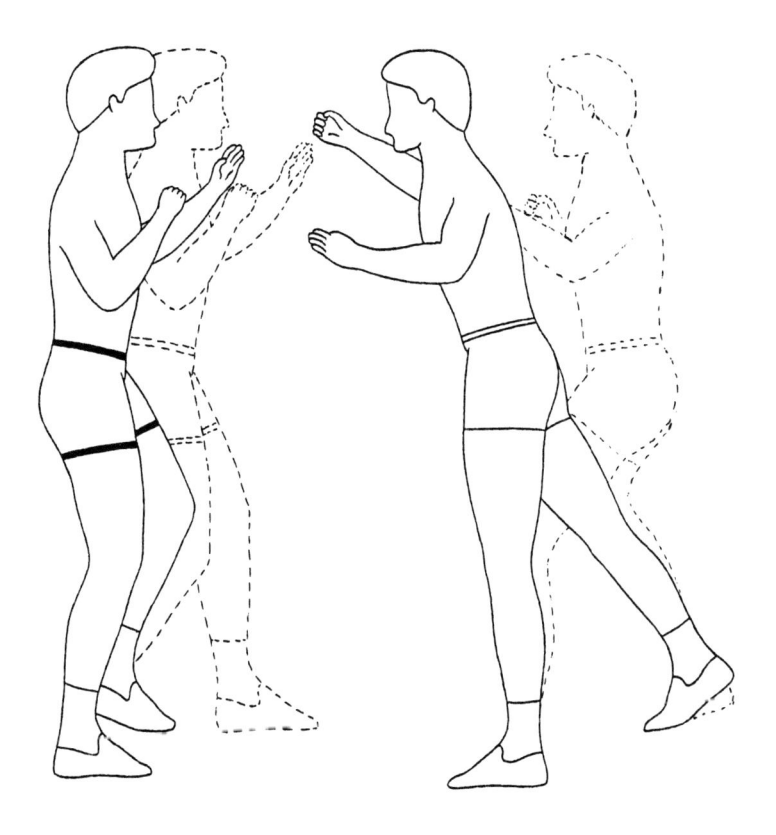

FIGURE 110

Figure 110. Your opponent begins an advance with a high, wide right-handed punch at your upper vertical gate. Shift your weight onto your right foot long enough to make the adjusting step depicted in the illustration.

▼

FIGURE 111

Figure 111. Stop the incoming blow with an inside suto block.

FIGURE 112

Figure 112. Take a full grip on the offending arm as shown. Shift your weight onto your left leg while pivoting 90 degrees. Chamber your right leg for a side kick.

▼

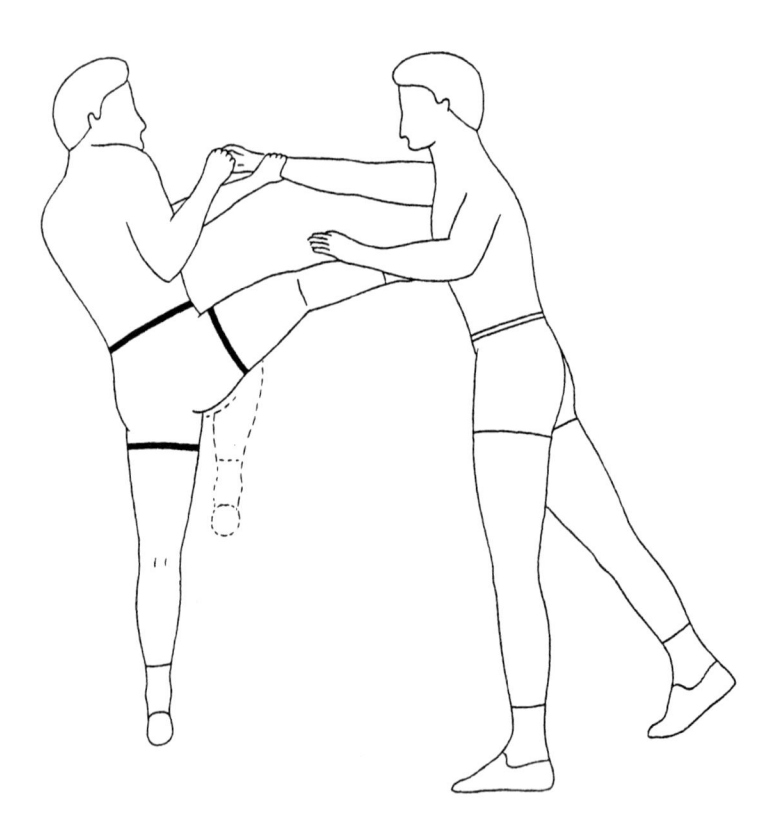

FIGURE 113

Figure 113. Your target is the solar plexus, but note that the leg is not fully locked into the side kick. If you fully locked the kick out you would likely push the opponent too far away to maintain your grip on his arm, thus allowing his body to travel beyond the range of your second kick. But this is not always so. It depends on the length of your arm and your opponent's, as well as the length of your leg. The kick is illustrated here in its shortened form for study purposes and to make the point that varying leg and arm lengths affect target proximities.

▼

FIGURE 114

Figure 114. From the weapon/target contact position in Figure 113, retract your leg to the roundhouse kick chamber position.

▼

FIGURE 115

Figure 115. Extend your roundhouse kick into your opponent's ear.

FIGURE 116

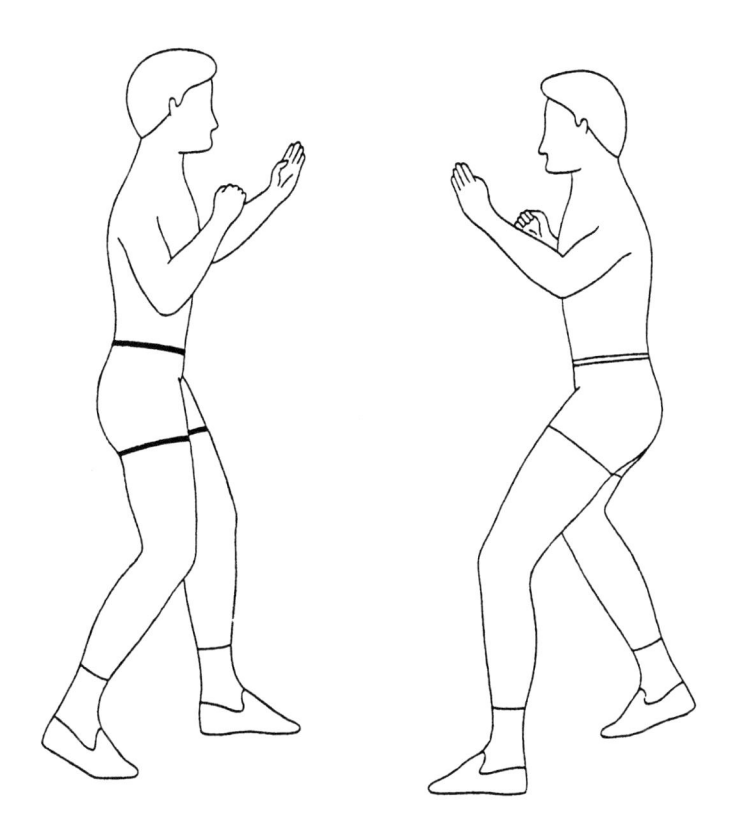

Figures 116 through 122
Figure 116. In this combination, we're going to use a combination side kick—one low and one high.

▼

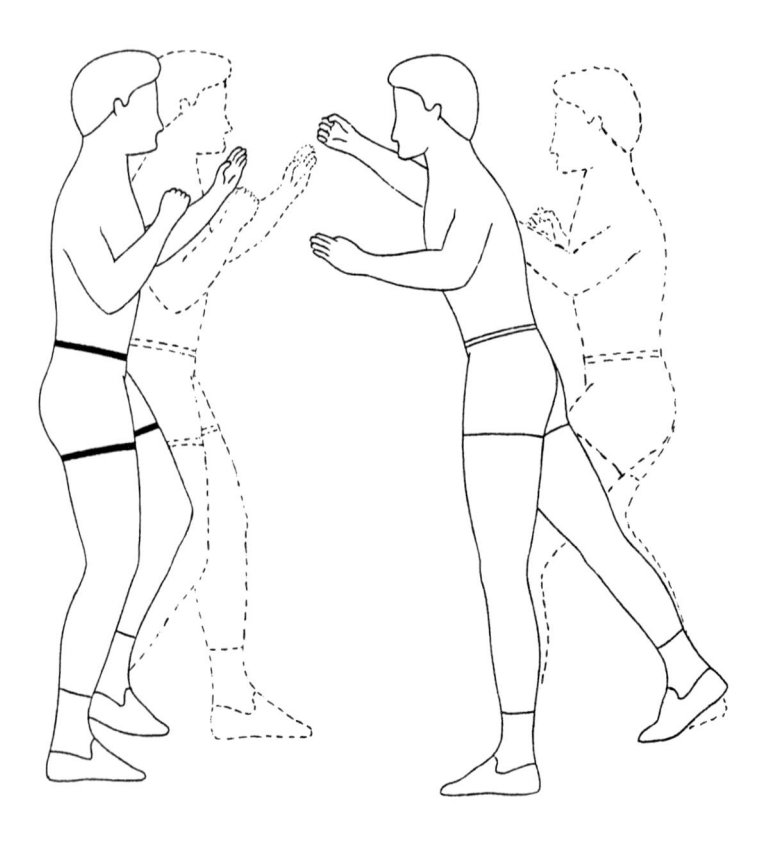

FIGURE 117

Figure 117. As your opponent advances with a right roundhouse punch, make your adjusting step with the left foot.

FIGURE 118

Figure 118. As your opponent's strike reaches its arc toward you, snap out your suto block.

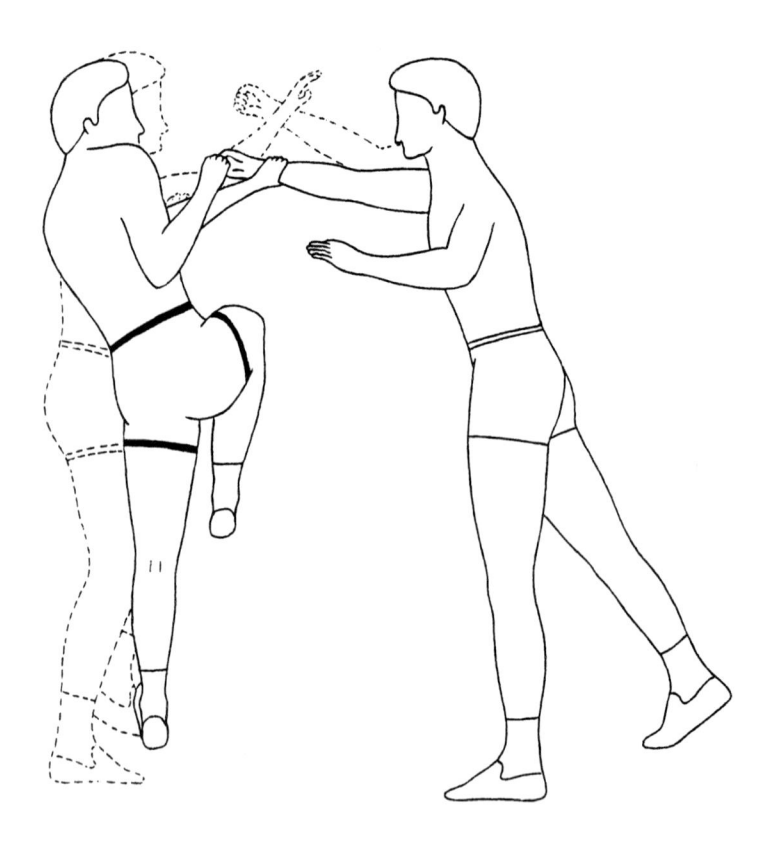

FIGURE 119

Figure 119. Take a full grip on the offending arm and shift your weight onto your left leg while pivoting counter-clockwise to ninety degrees. Chamber your right leg for a side kick.

▼

FIGURE 120

Figure 120. In this illustration, the opponent's left arm has been omitted to give you a better view of the shortened extension of the kick and the location of the anatomical target.

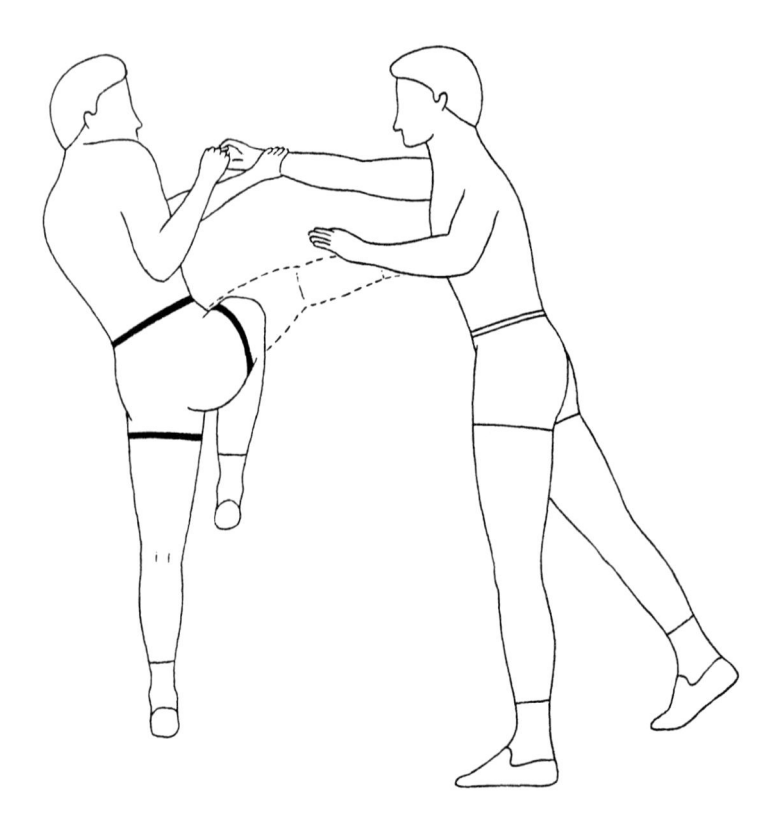

FIGURE 121

Figure 121. Maintaining your grip on the opponent's arm, chamber your right leg for another side kick.

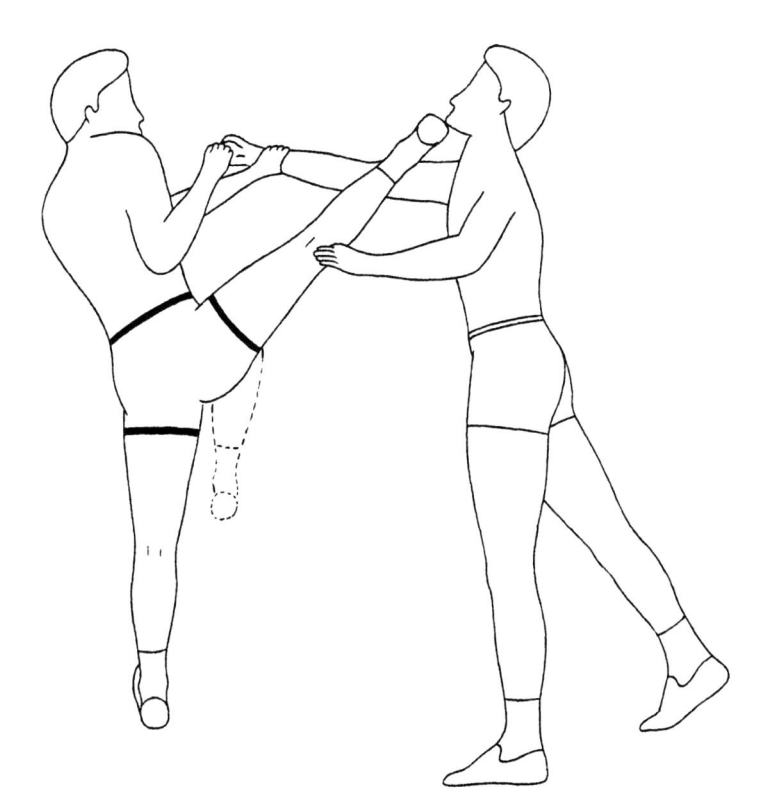

FIGURE 122

Figure 122. Lock your side kick fully out into the tip of your opponent's mandible. Note that at the same proximity, the side kick, when thrown at the higher target, is at perfect range with perfect penetration. The higher the kick, the closer the target must be.

▼

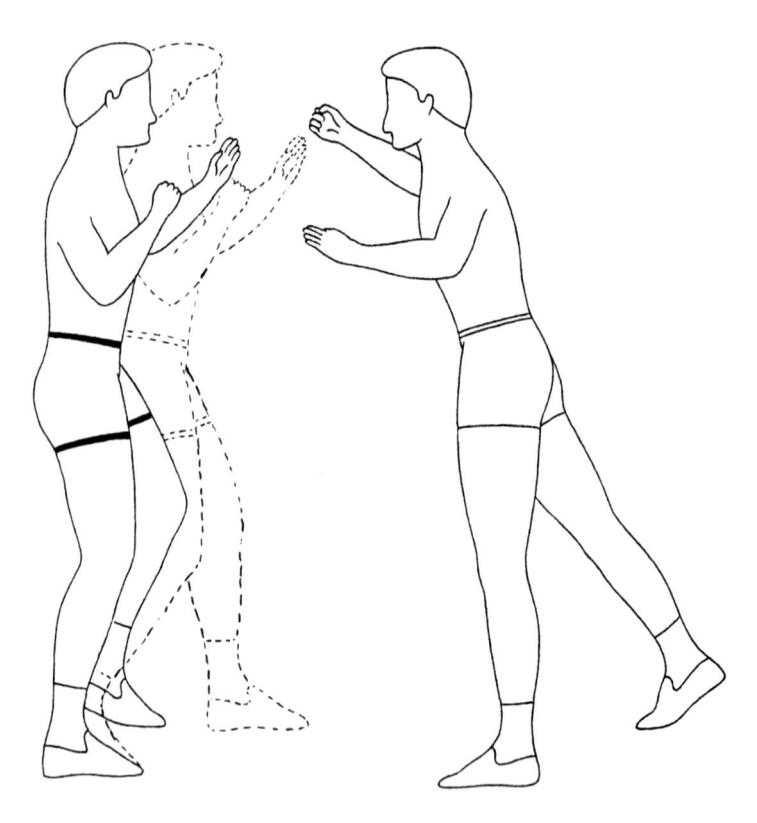

FIGURE 123

Figures 123 through 128

In this sequence we're going to attack a high target and then a low target, as opposed to the graduating heights of the kicks in the previous combinations. If you will look back to the sequence in Figures 109 through 115, you will find that the same two kicks were used in combination, but in the opposite order.

Figure 123. Your opponent advances with a high, wide right-handed punch at your upper vertical gate. Shift your weight onto your right leg long enough to make the adjusting step depicted by the dotted lines.

▼

FIGURE 124

Figure 124. Stop the incoming punch with a left inside suto block.

▼

FIGURE 125

Figure 125. Take a full grip on your opponent's arm at the wrist. Shift your weight onto your left leg while pivoting to ninety degrees, and chamber your right leg for a high roundhouse kick.

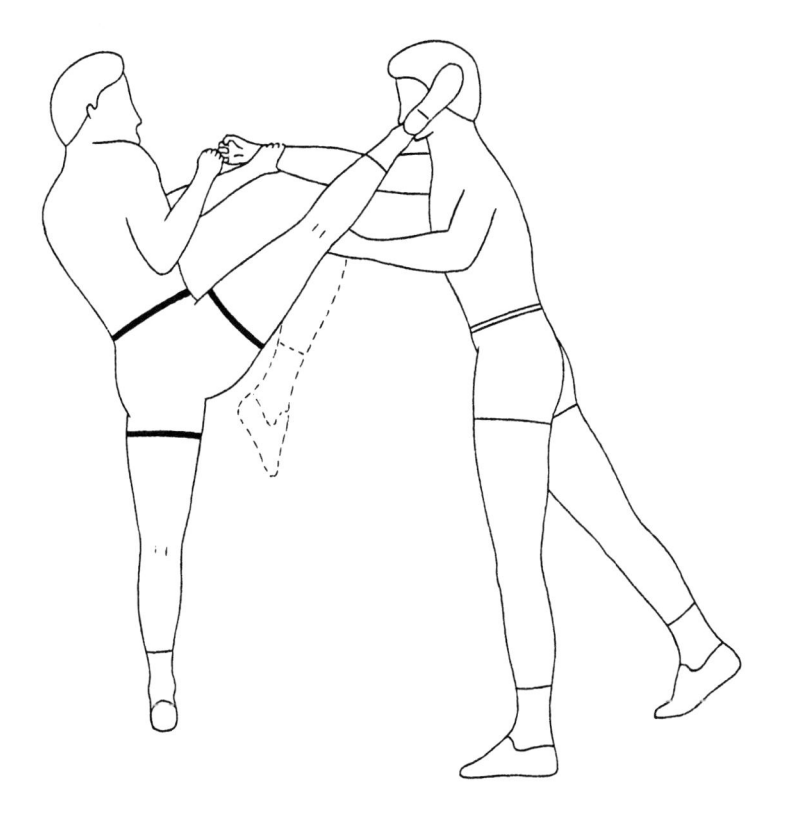

FIGURE 126

Figure 126. Extend your side kick into your opponent's ear while retaining your grip on the blocked arm.

▼

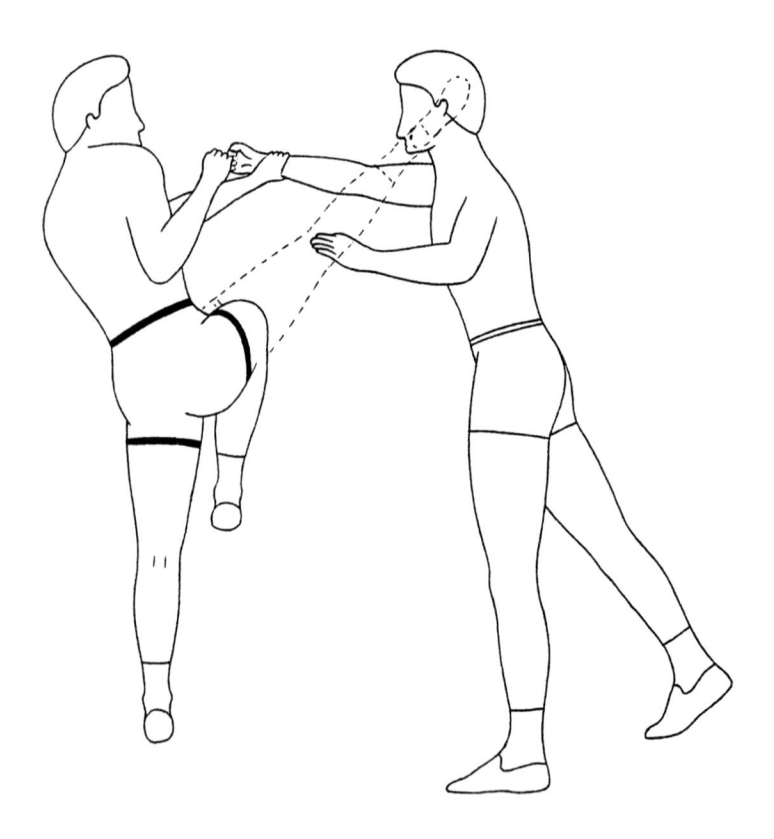

FIGURE 127

Figure 127. Retract your leg from the roundhouse kick directly to the side kick chamber position.

▼

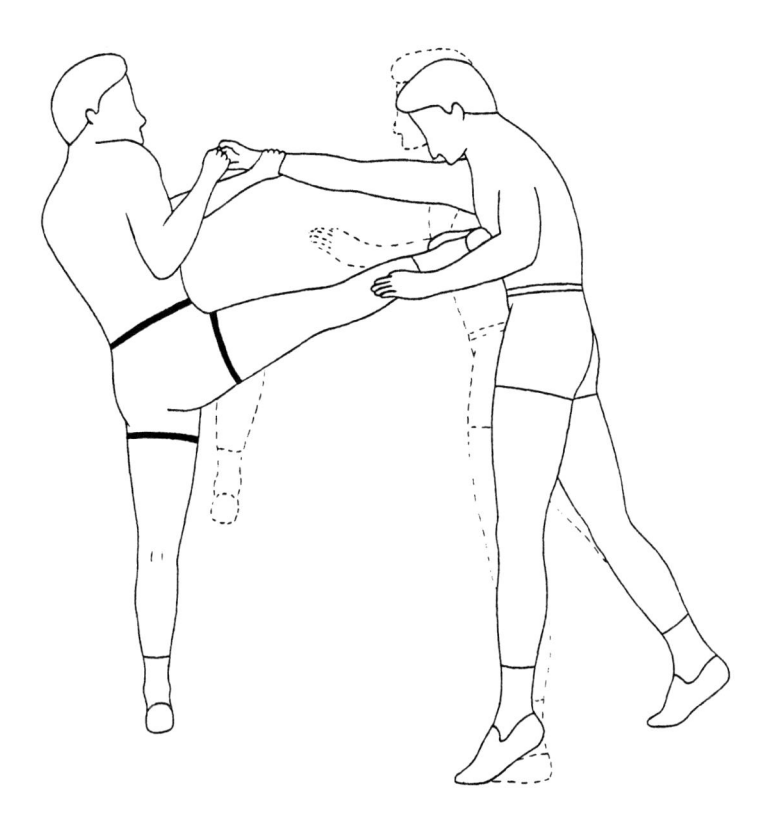

FIGURE 128

Figure 128. Lock your side kick into your opponent's solar plexus.

▼

FIGURE 129

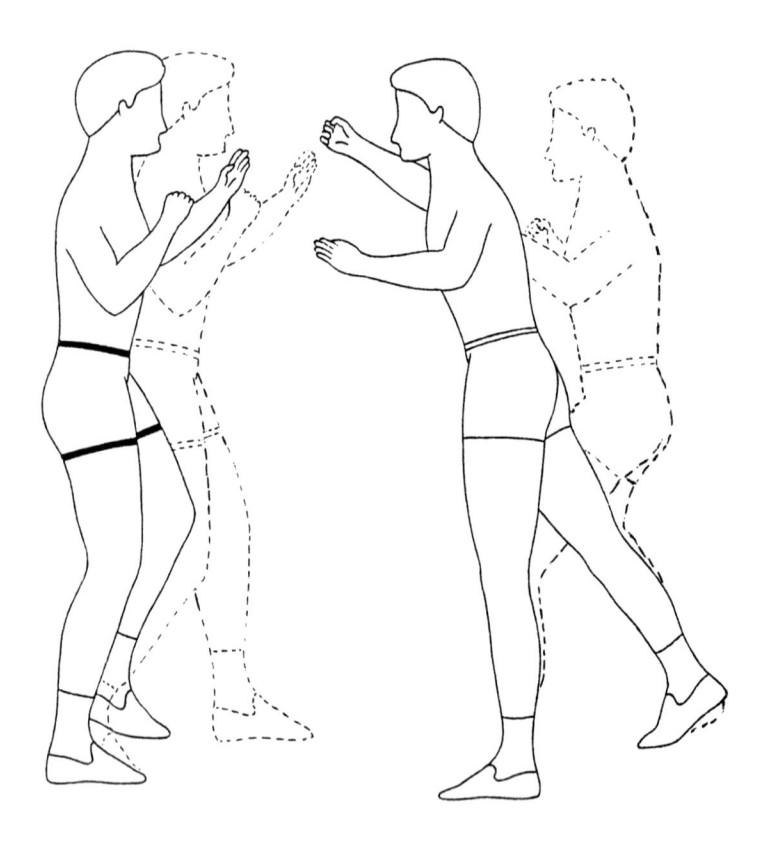

Figures 129 through 134
In this last sequence, we will combine the roundhouse and side kick again but aim at two high targets.

Figure 129. Your opponent begins a forward shift while initiating a high right roundhouse punch. Make your adjusting step with your left foot.

▼

FIGURE 130

Figure 130. With your left hand, stop the incoming blow with an inside suto block.

▼

FIGURE 131

Figure 131. Take a full grip on your opponent's punching arm at the wrist. Shift your weight back onto your left foot while pivoting to ninety degrees, and chamber your right roundhouse kick.

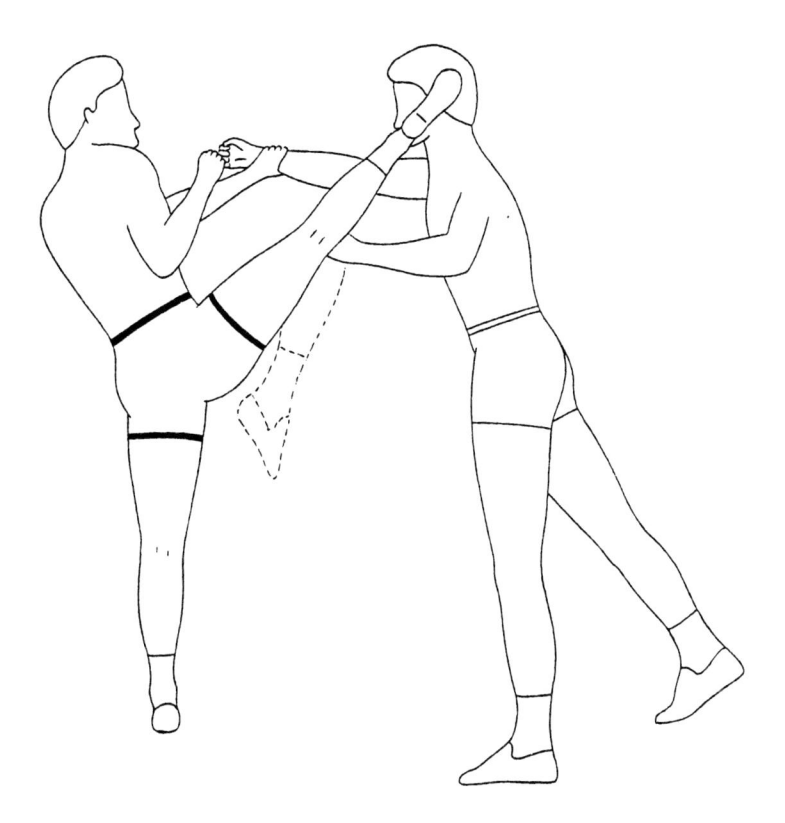

FIGURE 132

Figure 132. Snap out your roundhouse kick to your opponent's ear while maintaining your grip on his wrist.

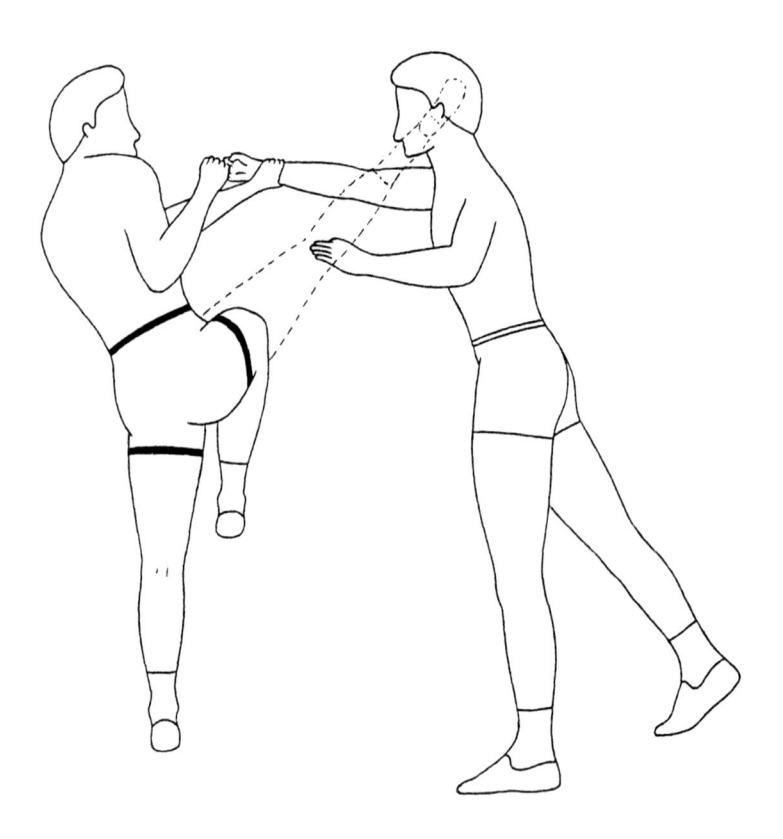

FIGURE 133

Figure 133. Keep the grip on your opponent's wrist and retract your kicking leg to the chamber position for a side kick.

FIGURE 134

Figure 134. Lock your side kick upward into the tip of your opponent's mandible.

CHAPTER SIX

HAND COMBINATIONS

Hand combinations are structurally faster than kicking combinations, simply because the distance the weapon must travel is generally shorter, requiring a shorter stroke. The appendage carrying the weapon with a hand strike (the arm) is shorter than the appendage carrying a kick (the leg). There is also the matter of proximity to be considered. The distance of an "in-range" gap for hand strikes is considerably less than that for kicks. However, there is a negative facet to the the delivery-time advantage: when you are in range to use hand weapons, so is your opponent; when your opponent is in range of your high-speed weapons, you are in range of his.

You should also be aware that the legs and hips can be used to generate power for hand strikes; the arms and shoulders cannot add power to kicks. Also, hand weapons, because they are small and may be formed into a number of shapes, are more effective when attacking smaller targets. Selecting weapons for specific targets under the numerous variables incidental to free-fighting is a process to be studied and practiced in the kwoon (school). When the confrontation is real, with real poten-

▼

FIGURE 135

tial for injurious consequences, the instincts and the mechanical operation of the defensive machine you are developing will conduct the fight for you. Therefore, how you train will be how you fight.

Figures 135 through 139

Figure 135. Your opponent is facing you in a side straddle position; you are in your standard ready position. We are going to use a scooping palm block with a suto and full-turn punch combination.

▼

FIGURE 136

Figure 136. Leading with his left foot and following with his right, your opponent advances with a mid-range half-turn punch.

▼

FIGURE 137

Figure 137. Redirect the incoming punch with a circular, counterclockwise movement of the left hand as shown. Rechamber the right hand to the high suto position.

▼

FIGURE 138

Figure 138. With a left-right sequential step, advance toward your opponent and deliver a palm-up suto to the base of the cranium. Retract the blocking hand to the chin-level chamber position.

▼

FIGURE 139

Figure 139. Extend a full-turn punch into the tip of your opponent's mandible.

FIGURE 140

Figures 140 through 145

Figure 140. In this combination, we will start from the same position and use the same block and first strike, but we will rechamber the right hand and use it again on another rear target.

▼

FIGURE 141

Figure 141. The opponent attacks with a left mid-range punch, again using a shuffle step to close the gap between you.

FIGURE 142

Figure 142. Using a scooping palm block, deflect the blow outside the width of your body and chamber your right hand to the suto position.

▼

FIGURE 143

Figure 143. Advance on your opponent with a left-right step, and strike the base of his cranium with a palm-up suto. Chamber your left hand at the chin as you deliver the strike.

FIGURE 144

Figure 144. Return the striking hand to the high suto position for the final stroke.

▼

FIGURE 145

Figure 145. Close the hand into a hammer fist and strike the left branch of your opponent's brachial plexus.

FIGURE 146

Figures 146 through 150

Figure 146. We will again defend against a side-straddled opponent launching a mid-range half-turn punch with his lead hand, but the block will differ from that of the previous technique.

▼

FIGURE 147

Figure 147. Your opponent lunges toward you, beginning a mid-range, left-handed half-turn punch.

▼

FIGURE 148

Figure 148. This right-handed palm block follows two lines: downward at 45 degrees and across your body at 45 degrees. As your hand makes contact with the incoming blow, clamp your fingers around the arm as you guide it away from your body. Close your left hand into a fist as you complete the block.

▼

FIGURE 149

Figure 149. Throw a short, left-handed half-turn punch to the tip of your opponent's mandible. As you are extending your left punch, your right hand should be en route to the high suto chamber position. As the punch lands, the suto is fully chambered.

▼

FIGURE 150

Figure 150. Snap your palm-up suto into the base of your opponent's cranium.

▼

FIGURE 151

Figures 151 through 155
Figure 151. In this sequence you'll face your opponent directly and use a suto/punch combination from a high-gate roundhouse punch attack.

▼

FIGURE 152

Figure 152. Your opponent leans forward, decreasing the gap between you, and begins a wide roundhouse punch directed at your upper vertical gate.

▼

FIGURE 153

Figure 153. Stop the incoming blow with a left inside suto block while chambering your right hand to the high suto position.

FIGURE 154

Figure 154. Strike your opponent's brachial plexus with a vertical suto while bringing your left hand to chamber at the chin.

▼

FIGURE 155

Figure 155. Extend a full-turn punch to the tip of your opponent's mandible.

FIGURE 156

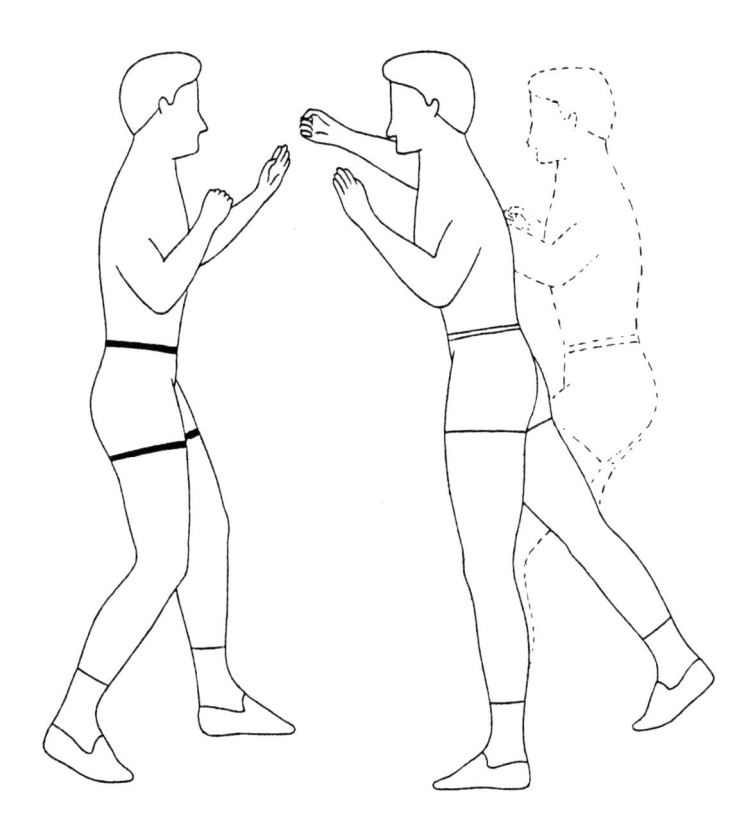

Figures 156 through 159

In this final sequence, you'll block a high-gate roundhouse punch with a crossing palm block and counter with combination half-turn punches.

Figure 156. Here your opponent initiates his forward motion and right-handed punch.

▼

FIGURE 157

Figure 157. Using your right hand, meet the incoming punch at the wrist with a crossing palm block.

▼

FIGURE 158

Figure 158. Strike your opponent at the tip of the mandible with a left half-turn punch while chambering your right-side punch to its ready position.

▼

FIGURE 159

Figure 159. Lock your right half-turn punch into the tip of your opponent's mandible again. Rechamber your left hand as your right punch extends.

▼